# Collecting for Tomorrow

# BOXES

## BRIAN COLE

**BPC PUBLISHERS LTD.**

Designed and produced by
Walter Parrish International Ltd., London


Printed and bound in Spain by
TONSA, San Sebastian
Dep. Legal: SS 439/82

ISBN 0 273 00235 X

# Contents

# Author's acknowledgements

My thanks are due to many people who so readily agreed to help and advise on this book. In particular I should like to thank Heather Jones and Jane Maitland Hudson, of Walter Parrish International, for their constant patience and good humour. My gratitude is also due to those collectors who so willingly allowed me to inspect their treasured 'boxes'; in particular to Mr and Mrs A. Ball and Mr and Mrs P. Wyer, also to Glennys Wild of the City Museum and Art Gallery, Birmingham, for her invaluable help. I must also thank Neville Smith and Yvette Cooper for services beyond the normal call of their duties, and my company, Phillips, for its ready co-operation.

# Introduction

Virtually everyone is a collector of boxes; many people are by choice, but the majority are collectors quite inadvertently. For most of us keep boxes, for the dressing table, for games, jewellery, clothing, tea, string or a myriad of other articles and thus quite unconsciously become collectors of boxes. Next time you look at these boxes, take a few moments to consider the box as a piece of craftsmanship in itself. Many will be crudely made, perhaps the work of a local craftsman or made by an amateur in his spare time, others may be mass produced to package an everyday product such as biscuits, and others will be small works of art in their own right. All these boxes have a historical background which makes their continued use today all the more fascinating and I have attempted to trace the backgrounds of as many types of boxes as possible.

Boxes have been made in virtually every material to be found and in almost every country of the world. Basically a box is a container used to protect objects from damage and to make them easily portable. So the first pieces of personal furniture ever made were boxes or coffers intended to convey the owner's goods and chattels, probably by mule, from place to place. From these humble beginnings derive, for instance, the superb gold boxes set with precious stones and enamels, favoured by Louis XV of France. These are extravagant works of art in themselves but they, like many boxes of today, were originally intended as gifts and tokens of goodwill. They still make sublime gifts, but for both the collector and giver, there are literally hundreds of less extravagant subjects. For boxes, perhaps more than any other collecting field, extend from the sublime to the ridiculous.

More serious collectors of boxes will recognize the need to establish a theme because of the thousands of types available. Collectors used to select a theme in material, e.g. enamels or silver, but today, there is a growing trend towards collecting special types of boxes and containers such as tobacco boxes, tea caddies and visiting-card cases.

This allows a much wider range in both price, style and material. In addition, a 'subject' collection has enormous value as a link with history. To give just one example, the snuff and sugar boxes of yesterday were treasured heirlooms, their contents were rare and the boxes often had locks. Now, throw-away mass-produced cardboard containers reflect how cheap and easily available their contents are.

A serious collector, having established some type of theme, will inevitably start buying boxes either from friends, antique shops or perhaps auctions. Indeed, the hunt and eventual acquisition is part of the excitement of collecting. The good collector will look at each objectively and ask himself a number of questions.

*a* Is it possible to give a date to the box on stylistic grounds?
*b* What is the construction of the box and the type of materials used?
*c* What was the purpose of the box?
*d* What is the decoration, if any, and is it original?

This set of questions, which may on occasions have simple answers, are the essential approach not only to boxes, but to antiques generally. A silver box may be well hallmarked and relatively easy to examine, but many silver snuff-boxes have been well used and through the years their contents may have worn away all or part of the marks, leaving the present owner with a dating problem. Alternatively, many small boxes were not marked at all, and perhaps could have emanated from France, Holland or America. Such are the interesting questions that may confront the collector.

The condition of a box is of course important, but do not necessarily reject a box because it is broken. If it cannot be repaired these boxes often can serve as examples of a type of material or construction and can often be just as instructive as a perfect example. Better still, they can often be bought at a fraction of the price of a good box!

This book has attempted to examine a wide range of everyday boxes from the point of view of style and materials, concentrating on boxes which are still readily available in antique shops and auctions and are consequently relatively inexpensive. Many have little commercial value at present and perhaps can still only be found by rummaging through an attic or old store house.

Mass-produced cardboard boxes have yet to assume any commercial value, but early ephemera of this type have an interesting role to play in the history of packaging as have their tin counterparts. Early biscuit boxes can make a colourful and attractive display, to mention just one example.

Some collectors may be the proud possessors of only three or four boxes, say for pens and pencils, pins and needles or some other purpose perhaps for which the box was not originally made. An old tea caddy may hold small flower decorations with wonderful effect. Casual collectors of boxes often have been given their boxes or acquired them for little at sales or second-hand shops. To them, I trust, this book will show that each box is in its own right a small piece of social history or perhaps, 'folk art', linking one era with another. Indeed, most boxes if treated reasonably have more permanence than their owners!

Whilst there are many books on fine expensive boxes there is little published material on the wealth of humble boxes that exist. To begin with, read as much as you can about other aspects of your chosen theme. Boxes are very personal possessions and almost always reflect current fashions. Learn to recognize materials: to be able to tell faience from porcelain, mahogany from varnished pine and, as you become more expert, the oriental lacquer from the European version is particularly important since small boxes were seldom marked, carefully or accurately, if at all, and a type of glaze or a kind of wood may give you a valuable clue.

Above all, clean your junk-shop finds carefully. It is unlikely that you will find gold and jewels under black enamel but it has been known to happen. More down-to-earth, rough handling can break the fragile construction of a hinge or scratch irreparably the pleasant painting under a coat of thick varnish.

The best general cleaning equipment is pure soap, an old, soft toothbrush and as little water as possible. Never leave wood in water, no matter how dirty.

# Glossary

APPLIED DECORATION: Ornament added to a box after its manufacture by soldering, pinning or by glue. Mostly used in metal, gemstones or in pottery and porcelain boxes.

BOULLE: Named after the 17th century French craftsman André Charles Boulle, a technique of marquetry using brass and stained tortoiseshell.

BOXWOOD: Hardwood particularly light in colour, used for wood turning or inlay.

BRASS: Alloy of copper and zinc much used in the production of cheap general-purpose boxes or to provide metal mounts or inlay.

CALAMANDER: Strongly marked hardwood often used for toilet and writing cases.

CAST DECORATION: Style of decoration often found on metal boxes to make intricate and detailed covers or panels by use of moulds.

CHASING: Style of decoration on metal akin to engraving but not producing the sharp 'cut' of the latter.

CLOISONNÉ: Enamel technique using fine wires to divide the enamels.

CROSSBANDING: Furniture technique found on larger boxes or caddies—a strip of wood veneer in contrast colour or figure to the main veneer.

DAMASCENE: Inlay of metal with gold or silver hammered into the body.

DÉCOUPAGE: A collage type decoration using cut outs from books, magazines etc.

DIE STAMPING: Repeated embossed decoration on boxes produced by a mechanical stamp.

ELECTRO PLATING: Process of deposition by electricity, of thin coat of silver onto a metal base, usually copper.

EMBOSSING OR REPOUSSÉ: Decoration raised from the surface of metal by hammering from the back.

ENAMELS: Vitreous process of fusing a glass-like substance to a base, usually of copper.

ENGINE TURNING: Lathe-turning operation to produce repetitive line engraving.

FRUIT WOOD: Wood from apple, pear and cherry, often used to make boxes, normally given this name by the trade.

HARDSTONES: Semi-precious stones such as agate, lapis lazuli, onyx or malachite.

LACQUER: Finest work comes from Japan using the lac of the sumac tree.

MARQUETRY: Delicate inlay with patterns, usually of wood in wood.

MOSAIC: Pattern produced by gluing small stones on glass tiles together to form a pattern or picture.

MOSS AGATE: Greenish stone having a moss or seaweed like pattern used for box panels.

MULL: Scottish snuff-box made by mounting a small curled horn.

NIELLO: Black metal alloy used on engraved boxes to give contrast to metal, particularly favoured on Russian boxes.

PEWTER: Alloy of lead and tin, used for tobacco and snuff-boxes in particular.

PIETRA DURA: Hardstone or marble used occasionally as decoration on covers or panels simulating fruit or flowers.

SCRIMSHAW: Carving in whalebone, especially of American whalers.

SHAGREEN: Untanned leather of horse or often sharkskin mostly dyed green, used to cover some boxes of wood frames.

SHEFFIELD PLATE: Copper covered by thin layer of silver by a rolling technique, used for cheap boxes to imitate silver.

STUMPWORK: Elaborate raised embroidery using various materials and raised by stumps of wood or pads of wool.

TRANSFER PRINTING: Mechanical technique used on wood, pottery, porcelain, tin and papier-mâché boxes, to imitate the more expensive hand-painted decoration.

# Salt boxes

Salt boxes are very often of an indeterminable date since they have been in common use in kitchens for centuries. Salt requires a container to keep it dry, and therefore, by custom, it has been kept in boxes hanging near the fireplace. The salt box is often still a common sight in country houses and farmhouses, and is most often found made of wood; oak is particularly popular. In America, pine and maple were used. Because of the corrosive quality of salt, metal nails were not often used in the manufacture of these wooden boxes. They were made by joinery and by means of dowels. Most were rectangular in shape with a slightly sloping front forming the lid which was hinged at the back. The boxes had a back plate made with an aperture, to fix the box to the wall. Some which were intended to stand on the kitchen table had compartments for both rock salt and granulated salt.

Such boxes are commonplace throughout Europe and America, and since they were made by local craftsmen, or even by a member of the family or staff, there are virtually as many variations in decoration as there are boxes. They range in size from around 6 inches in width to 15 or 16 inches, and most rely on 'chip carving' with a mallet and chisel for their decoration. The style of decoration should give the collector some idea of date.

The use of a stylized motif such as a Tudor rose, roundels and flowerheads, suggests a date from 1660 to 1720. Sometimes these boxes have a date carved on them, although this may not always be taken to be the actual date of manufacture. Boxes with inlaid decoration in wood often date from the period 1770 to 1820.

Salt boxes can also be found in Tunbridge Ware, or painted in the bright colours common to European peasant arts and crafts. They are also often found in other materials; pewter is quite common, for instance, and these boxes probably date from the latter part of the 16th century. Salt boxes of Delftware and pottery are also not uncommon, as both these materials are well suited to the purpose.

*Carved wooden salt boxes, the top one 10 inches wide and marked with the date 1728; English, 18th century.*

# Cutlery and candle boxes

These are somewhat akin to salt boxes and are often mistaken for them because of their similarly upright shape. Their original use was for storing everyday knives and forks in the kitchen. The wooden bodies often taper sharply towards the bottom and have a small hinged flap which forms the cover. They were usually made in well-figured wood which would show up distinctly on the front panel, or alternatively they would have a decorative inlay. Mahogany and oak were the most popular woods used for cutlery boxes, which were in general use in England and America during most of the 18th century and well into the 19th. Many American examples are in native woods; pine, maple, etc.

Spoons and cutlery were also kept in small kitchen racks, often made in the shape of a miniature kitchen dresser. Like the cutlery boxes, they were hung on the wall; the bottom compartment formed a box for the general cutlery, whilst the racks normally held the spoons. This type of hanging box is often mistakenly called a candle box, but candle boxes are usually rectangular in shape with a removable top cover which slides into its holding grooves. Both kinds are often very simply made of common woods, although some examples may be more attractively finished, with moulded borders.

Candle boxes were mostly made in mahogany and occasionally have more than one division, often two, one used as a store for the tinder. Brass and pewter are other materials used for candle boxes which can still be seen in use in country houses and farmhouses.

Rush-light boxes may also occasionally be found. In general, these do not have covers, and are plain, wall-hanging boxes intended to hold wax-covered rushes—a form of lighting almost as old as history. They continued to be used well into the 20th century, adapted as spillholders for lighting fires.

*Mahogany and satinwood cutlery box, 15 inches high; English, late 18th century.*

# Shaker

Boxes made by the Shaker community in the 19th century are much sought after by American collectors. This austere sect was founded by Mother Ann Lee who was born in England, and, after imprisonment, left for the American Colonies in 1774. Here with her small band of followers she settled in Watervliet, New York, to farm and practise religion. The Shakers' philosophy imposed a strict moral discipline based on hard work, celibacy and devotion to God. 'Hands to work and hearts to God' was their guiding motto. By 1860 the community had grown to about 6000 and they had settled in New England, New York, Ohio and Kentucky. The Shakers actually invented many conveniences still employed today in the home and on the farm.

Their puritan life-style was reflected in their furniture and accessory designs which were entirely plain without any detailed carving or inlay, and devoid of cross-banding or veneer. The wood itself was the only decoration or occasionally a vegetable dye paint was used. The sect believed it received direct divine inspiration which led them to make the plain useful furniture and accessories collected today. Windsor chairs with rushed seats, beds, chests, and utility boxes were made not only for the communities themselves but for sale to the outside world. Their boxes were well constructed with much attention given to craftsmanship. Shaker candle boxes, vegetable boxes, and culinary boxes are much sought after today. They were functional boxes, constructed mainly from maple wood, old pine or fruit wood and some are found together in nests, and occasionally one can still come across a box with a name label.

The communities eventually dwindled until only a handful of believers remained. Today several old Shaker villages have been restored and maintained and here we can absorb the environment which produced such dedicated workmanship.

*Two Shaker boxes, the top one 5 inches long, and a small burl carved snuff box; American, c. 1870.*

# Kitchen and store boxes

Wooden boxes have been used in kitchens for centuries, many being home-made with crude decoration, if any at all. The small, hanging salt box shown is sparsely decorated with hot-poker work. This type of decoration, together with gouging and chip-carving, is very common in this sort of box.

In the Middle Ages spices had their place alongside precious metals, such as gold and silver, as some of the most highly-prized commodities in the western world. Although they were freely found in India and China, the long and treacherous journey from the Far East made them expensive and rare in the West.

Spices were traditionally kept under lock and key in small cupboards that looked like miniature chests of drawers. Some 17th century boxes were made with radiating divisions with screw-on lids to keep them airtight. This type of box would often have a grater in the centre compartment. In the 19th century sets of turned-wood boxes or nests were used for spice storage, many of them bearing the names of individual spices. Others took the form of hanging boxes with named drawers. Small boxes to contain a nutmeg and grater were made for both kitchen and pocket use. Bentwood storage boxes were produced by steaming a single-ply strip of wood around a shaped base, usually oval or round, and many early examples were made without nails but rather by means of joinery and wooden pegs. They were fitted with tight lids and made excellent kitchen containers. Later spice and storage boxes appeared in japanned metal and tin, and examples with printed decoration or wording date from 1900 onwards. Some earlier ones are to be found which were in general use in food stores to dispense tea etc., in small quantities to customer's requirements.

*Kitchen containers for salt in pine and pottery; diameter of pot 5 inches; American, mid-19th century.*

# Knife boxes

From the early part of the 18th century onwards, the table cutlery used for important occasions was kept in special boxes which stood on the sideboard. The finest cutlery had mounts and handles in porcelain, enamels, or finely-chased metal, and to preserve the cutlery, the maker would supply it in a suitable box, often of the type shown. Most knife boxes are to be found in wood, and incorporate a sloping, hinged cover enclosing a pierced panel to retain the cutlery, with a serpentine-shaped front, and small bracket feet. They often incorporate inlaid decoration and have contemporary silver mounts. The silver hallmarks of English examples can be used as a general guide to the date of manufacture. The sloping front of the cover was often used to contain an oval panel of marquetry or inlay decoration in contrasting woods.

Although most knife boxes followed this conventional shape, some can be found in the form of the classical urns which were made so popular by the Adams Brothers. They date from 1780 to 1800, and were designed to be used on sideboards of a neo-classical design. They were usually in veneered woods, often satinwood, and had a rising cover secured by a central dowel through the urn cover. The cover had panels of inlaid wood in box, ebony, holly, and others. Sometimes stained woods were used to add colour. Knife boxes fell out of custom about 1820, and from this date the sideboard was designed to include a separate cutlery drawer.

*George III mahogany knife box, inlaid; English, 12 inches high, 1800.*

# Transfer prints

Some of the earliest available forms of commercial packaging are the colourful 'pot lid' boxes produced from the 1840s onwards to contain bear's grease, fish-paste, toothpaste, potted meats etc.

The principal English manufacturers in Staffordshire were F. and R. Pratt of Fenton, together with Meyer and Company, Burslem, and the Cauldron Pottery Company, Shelton. Although most covers are unmarked, one may sometimes come across a box or lid bearing the name 'Pratt', or 'Pratt and Co.' The lids are unhinged, and loose-fitting. The bases are made from the same pottery as the lids and make ideal containers for creams and pastes. They are mainly circular in shape, but a number are simply rectangular, or rectangular with trefoil design on both lid and base. The earliest lids date from the period 1840 to 1850, and are normally small and quite flat. Later lids and box covers were slightly rounded in surface, and were relatively free from crazing or firing cracks.

The pictorial lids were produced by a transfer printing process which fixed the colour through five stages of printing. The finished lid was finally glazed and fired. The process required a high degree of technical skill.

There are some rare subjects, with captions such as 'Washington crossing the Delaware', or 'The Buffalo Hunt', both of which bear the name of H. P. and W. C. Taylor, perfumers of Philadelphia—thought to have been commissioned for their stand at the Philadelphia Exhibition in 1876—and then more common ones intended for fish paste entitled 'The Shrimpers', 'Hauling in the Trawl', or 'Mending the Nets'. The fishing and shrimping scenes often show children catching shrimps, or busy scenes of fishing boats hauling in their trawling nets in rough seas.

Most scenes depict landscapes with figures, and often bear titles, but there is a series of portraits of which some of the more commonly found are 'The Late Prince Consort', a seated study of Prince Albert; and 'The Later Duke of Wellington'.

*Selection of Staffordshire jars decorated with underglaze colour transfer printing: potted meat jars, including 'Duke of Wellington' tobacco jar 3 inches in diameter with simulated malachite ground (top and second row); rouge jars (third row) and toothpaste jars (bottom row); all English, 1850-70.*

# Cardboard

Cardboard boxes have not yet achieved the esteem they probably deserve in the eyes of collectors but this time must surely come. Cardboard boxes, or as they were known in the 19th century, paper boxes, reflect not only the commercial growth of our nations, their packaging and printing, but also the growing social revolution of the working class, who could now afford packaged foodstuffs and materials.

Naturally, most early packages have perished because of the nature of their material and lack of commercial value. In the early days most packaging took the form of paper bags and the most common items sold in this manner were tobacco and tea. These bags bore the name of the individual shopkeepers who sold them. Commercial paper-bag making dates from the mid 1850s. The first-known commercial box-making firm was established in London in 1817 and was still trading a century later. In America it was the European settlers who established the first box-making companies. Early boxes were oval or round in shape; hats, chocolates, fruits, collars and pills were ideal subjects for this type of packaging. Lithographic printing was also developing alongside the growing box-making industry to provide better printing on the outside of the box. Early boxes were unsuitable for direct printing and were covered with glued-on printed designs.

One development was in providing retailers with ready-made boxes which were creased and partially cut by machinery and which could be stored easily. This process was developed mainly in America in the 1880s and machines were exported to associated companies in England and other European countries.

Early cardboard packaging was used for phonographic cartridges, candles and cigarettes. Advertisements on them first appeared at the turn of the 20th century. These were the first to give pictorial representation of their own packaged products. Some interesting comparisons here can be made with modern packaging designs. The American Cereal Company produced a Quaker Oats package similar in design to those in use today and many old-established firms still maintain some old packaging styles.

*Two early printed cardboard packages, the top one 3 inches wide; American, 1900.*

# Games boxes

For centuries boxes have been made in all kinds of materials to contain playing cards and other games. Wood and leather boxes are common containers for playing cards, the leather varieties often displaying heavy gilt tooling as decoration. Tin, horn, papier-mâché, lacquer and bone containers are frequently found. Quite elaborate silver playing-card boxes have been made from the end of the 19th century for bridge and whist and sometimes these incorporate a marker or trump-card indicator on the cover.

Horn is one of the oldest and most primitive of materials in general use. It was essential in the Middle Ages to provide drinking cups and goblets. This use was revived to a limited extent in the 18th and 19th centuries. Small boxes in horn for dominoes and dice or horn diary- and card-cases are still often cheaply found.

Bone is another readily available material for inexpensive products. It is, of course, closely allied to ivory and many bone items are copies from expensive ivory products. Some of the finest bonework was produced by prisoners of war held mainly during the Napoleonic Wars (1793-1815). Prisoners were permitted to sell their work in order to improve their food and conditions, and they produced beautiful, fully-rigged miniature men-of-war, not to mention working models of guillotines! Prisoners also made boxes for games. Chess sets and draughts were produced in bone complete with outer boxes. Dominoes with painted spots were another favourite. Complete sets of playing cards with decoration painted onto the bone can still be found. Another popular game of the period was cribbage and the marking boards and card boxes were often made of bone.

From the Regency period onwards, games compendiums were made which look rather like stationery or toilet boxes. These are often fitted with stained-ivory chess, draughts or backgammon sets, comprising playing pieces and boards.

*Selection of games boxes: horn domino box, $2\frac{1}{2}$ inches long (top right), cut-porcupine-quill game box (top left), and wooden inlaid cribbage board (centre); all c. 1900.*

# Games and puzzles

Few Victorian middle-class houses were without a dolls-house for the girls whilst the boys played with train sets which originated in Germany in the last quarter of the 19th century.

Many collectors are now concentrating on preserving our grandparents' toys and games. Many boxes originally containing games have survived from this period and retain their fascination for us today.

Mah-Jong, a complicated game from China, was popular and many fine boxes were made to contain the ivory tiles. Most of these are made from Chinese hardwoods. The tiles themselves were beautifully engraved in coloured designs. In the late 1930s and 40s, there was a great revival in America so beware of cheap, badly-made sets imported then. Jigsaw puzzles or 'dissected pictures', as they were first known, appeared in the mid-19th century. They were sold in varnished boxes with sliding covers each of which had a printed paper label showing the maker's name and the title of the puzzle. They often had a moral or an historical theme. Well-designed boxes for backgammon, chess and draughts can still be found, often incorporating inlaid playing boards. Fell and Hammer, Lotto, Halma, all are forgotten Victorian games which may still be found in junkshops, flea markets or attics, often in their original cardboard boxes.

Boxes of building bricks sometimes doubling as puzzles were popular. The puzzle cubes were covered with printed paper which formed a picture, when put together. Each side of the cube could be used to make a separate picture and quite often this picture was repeated on the box cover.

Toys of painted tin were produced, the better ones being made mainly in Germany. Toy theatres, magicians' boxes and the famous Zoetrope (or wheel of life) are intriguing items to collect today. The latter was the forerunner of the movie-film and in the USA they cost one dollar in 1890. Model soldiers in their original boxes (e.g. those produced by William Britain from 1893 onwards) are much sought after today.

Boxes which are puzzles in themselves are common and are often fine examples of a box-maker's skill; the puzzle dice-box shown is a good example. By sliding the five-dot section one is then able to slide the four-dot side to reveal the miniature contents—quite a work of art!

*Selection of games and puzzle boxes: paper-covered box with interchangeable picture blocks (top), 8″ long; puzzle dice box (below); American, early 20th century.*

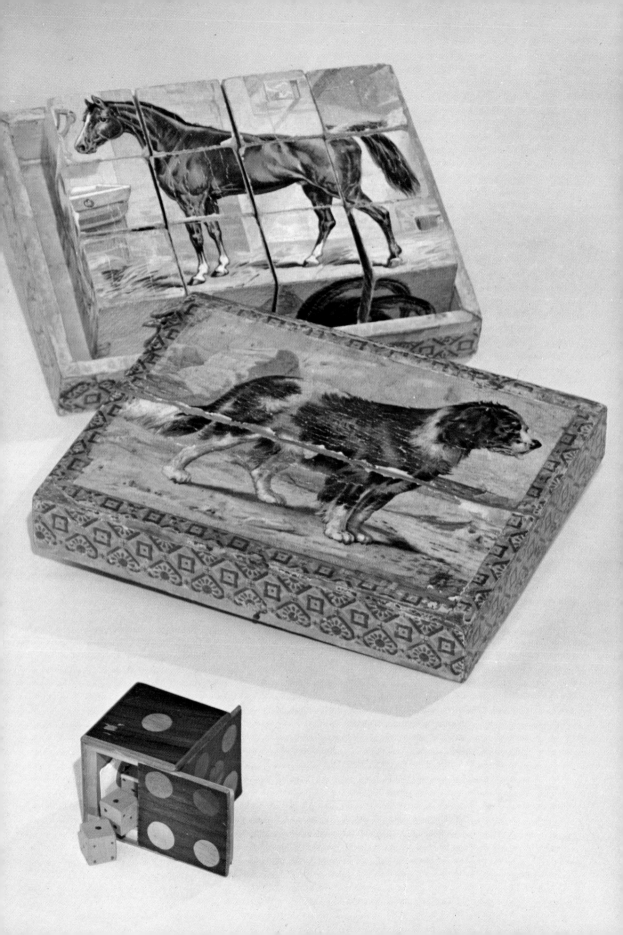

# Faience

Majolica, faience, and delftware are three varieties of one of the oldest types of ceramic ware, as popular today as they were centuries ago when they were first produced in their respective European countries. All three are a type of tin-glazed ware. When oxide of tin was added to the glaze, the first firing produced a very hard, brittle, and opaque surface which was much thicker than the earlier type, and completely covered the body and provided a background for painted decoration which was fired a second time. This is common to many glazed wares from southern and northern Europe, and is still used for utility articles and souvenirs.

Majolica is the earliest form, reaching its peak in the 15th to 16th century in Spain and Italy. The shapes, often in relief, were heavy and crude, with darkish tones of green, blue, orange, yellow, and some red. The general style was revived in Victorian England and America. Italian majolica boxes with figures and cupids in relief are still popular today.

The most renowned of all tin-glazed wares are from the Netherlands, commonly called delftware. Delft was in fact only one of many centres of production. Every town had its own potteries producing the famous blue-and-white wares and later bright polychrome ware. It is the nearest that European potters came to reproducing Oriental porcelain in a non-porcelain material, and this skill, together with the world trading power of the Dutch with their large empire in the 17th century, guaranteed commercial success and fame for the Dutch potters.

Tin-glazed wares which were produced in France and Germany were known by the generic term faience. Blue and white is always the most common combination since blue was the easiest colour to fix in ceramics and was produced from cobalt. The vividness of other colours was often lost during the firing process. Decoration of more than one colour, i.e. polychrome decoration, is usually blue, green or yellow often combined with an iron red. North European polychrome decoration is stylized and follows conventional patterns of floral designs, scrolls and exotic birds. The painting is glazed and fired at a high temperature. Many boxes bear a maker's mark. A great deal of tin-glazed ware was manufactured in the 19th century all over Europe and attractive pieces are still produced today.

*Biscuit box with plated mount, $8\frac{1}{2}$ inches long; European, c. 1920.*

# Money boxes

Since most money boxes were intended to be used by children, some charming and amusing ones were made and many still exist to be collected. Pottery, iron, wood and latterly tin are the most popular of the materials used for them.

The pottery example shown is a Prattware money box, made in Staffordshire by Pratt & Co. around 1800. The article was made from a mould and shows two children looking out of the top windows for the person hiding around the corner of the cottage. Other moulds of this type from the same factory principally take the shape of Wesleyan chapels, castles and houses. The author has recently seen a Pratt money box moulded in the shape of a grandfather clock. In the 'house' money boxes, the coins were inserted through a slot in the back of the roof and had to be extracted with the aid of a knife. Identical moulds were used to make pastille burners which explains why the chimneys may be out of proportion. Bright-coloured enamels usually added appeal to the boxes. The vivid cobalt blues, canary yellows and ochre browns would have brightened the eyes of many children in the early 19th century.

Money boxes in cast iron are also found in the shape of houses. The bank box shown opposite is made in cast iron with mounts in cut brass and is about 9 inches in height. It dates from the 1880s. Other collectable cast-iron boxes include the series of American examples which show the head and shoulders of a figure with an open hand in which to place the coin. When one presses a small lever, the coin passes through the figure's mouth into safe-keeping. Another amusing form is of a Negro figure with a donkey cart which tips up. The model has the name 'Bad Accident'. These boxes date from the latter part of the 19th century and very often still bear their original bright-coloured paintwork.

Boxes in wood are most commonly simply rectangular in form, fitted with a lock. These often have inlay work or mounts around the coin aperture or lock. More collectable are the wooden boxes, often apprentice-made pieces, made in the shape of a piece of furniture, i.e. a table or a chest of drawers. Small boxes with iron bandings and shaped like antique coffers or dower chests are, in fact, mostly old offertory or alms boxes.

*Staffordshire pottery money box, 6 inches high; English, 1820-40; and brass and iron money box; English, 1875.*

# Musical boxes

Music produced by mechanical methods was a leading source of home entertainment during the 19th century, in much the same way as the record player is today. Indeed, the homely musical box with its later development, the upright disc musical box, was the forerunner of the modern jukebox.

Musical boxes of the 19th century, which are readily collectable today, are primarily of the early cylinder type which was mainly superseded by the later disc musical box for table-top use. Both types require the mechanical striking of the teeth of a tuned metal musical comb in a pre-arranged sequence to give a required tune. This is combined with a motor drive to revolve the cylinder or disc. Table musical boxes have always been contained in handsome wooden cases. Many of the early boxes from the period 1850 to 1890 were contained in rosewood cases with strong figuring in the wood and often incorporating floral marquetry on the cover. The cylinder musical box industry was centred in Switzerland and was dominated by the firm Nicole Frères. Such boxes had the obvious fault of only being able to play a very limited amount of music and although improvements were made to cylinder boxes, of which the most important was the invention of interchangeable cylinders, the intro- duction of the disc-playing box soon tolled the death-knell for the cylinder type.

The first disc-playing musical boxes were produced by the Symphonion company, founded in Leipzig, Germany, by Paul Loch- mann in 1885. This company, Polyphon and Regina were the three main manufacturers of the industry which thrived in the period 1890 to 1914. The musical comb was played by means of either projections or holes in the discs, which were of mild steel or zinc and were readily interchangeable; in later years an automatic changing device was added. This was before the development of the phonograph and many automatic disc musical boxes, some worked by the coin-in-the- slot method, remain in use today having survived their terms of public entertainment in taverns.

Both Polyphon and Regina were founded by the German, Gustav Brachhausen. He founded Regina in New Jersey in 1894 after emigrating to America. Here he was a great success and was responsible for the manufacture of tens of thousands of musical boxes before they met their demise, superseded by the new-fangled talking machine.

*Disc table musical box in a rosewood case, 13 inches wide; German, c. 1900.*

# Tobacco boxes

Since about 1565, when tobacco was first introduced to Europe, craftsmen have made containers suitable for it. Such boxes had to maintain a level of humidity to preserve the essential aroma of the tobacco.

Tobacco jars were produced in many materials, glazed earthenware being one of the most common, and 'delft' blue-and-white designs were very popular. They were made by many Staffordshire factories from 1840 to 1870 and were normally cylindrical in shape with a removable lid and were rarely marked. Their decoration usually took the form of a coloured glaze, the favourites being tortoiseshell and simulated marble. A Pratt tobacco jar is shown opposite page 22.

Although many earthenware jars were produced between 1840 and 1870, it was the lead, pewter, and brass jars that were the most popular and effective. The lead varieties were mostly made for home or inn use, whilst most brass and pewter boxes were intended for pocket use. Tobacco boxes in lead date back to the middle of the 17th century and were particularly popular from 1750 to 1870. They were cast, often octagonal in shape, with a removable cover and were similar in appearance to contemporary tea caddies. Although their decoration is sparse, the knops on the lids are usually worthy of a collector's attention, as they so often take the form of a well-known figure of the day, and can help in dating the piece. Moulded lead boxes may have further scrolled or foliage decoration on the side panels and may even be cast with a coat of arms. Many were painted, but since the material was not really suitable for this, most boxes will only bear traces of the original paintwork. A common and rather macabre box, popular in the first half of the 19th century, was the coffin-shaped tobacco box.

Pocket tobacco boxes were made in precious metals and many emanate from Holland, which was not only a successful maritime nation but also a nation of craftsmen who devoted their skill to making fine boxes with elaborately-chased rustic scenes and views of country life in the style of the Dutch Old Masters. Many cheaper types were made in brass with similar designs. English silver and brass tobacco boxes of the same period are invariably plain or sparsely decorated. American tobacco boxes were made and advertised by a number of companies; most were fairly simple, with etched or bright-cut designs.

*Brass tobacco box, 3 inches in diameter; American, c. 1850 (top). Unusual leather tobacco box, 3 inches in diameter; American, 1880 (bottom).*

# Cigarette boxes

While cigarette smoking has been popular for centuries, the manufactured cigarette we know today was not produced until around
1850. The slide carton in cardboard, which makes the conventional
cigarette packet, first appeared in the 1890s—the first recorded were
those produced in 1892 for Wills's Three Castle cigarettes in Bristol.
These were an immediate success, as one of the previous problems
had been protecting the cigarettes from damage. This last point,
incidentally, led to the introduction of cigarette cards which were first
used to stiffen the paper packages. By 1900 cigarette cartons were
mass produced in Europe and America by individual factories on
contract to the tobacco companies. Tins holding 100 cigarettes were
also in common use, the tins being decorated either by transfer
printing or stuck-on paper labels.

Decorative cigarette boxes have been made in profusion since
smoking became an acceptable social habit and more particularly
when it became acceptable for women to smoke. The boxes illustrated show a range of leather, lacquer and enamel boxes. The red
lacquer is a common imitation of old carved Chinese lacquer and is
produced by a pressed process. This type of box is still frequently
found posing as a genuine Chinese lacquer box in some antique
shops. The black enamel pocket case shown dates from the 1920s
when plain enamel was popular. The cover is set with a rhinestone.
Table cigarette boxes in cedarwood with an outer casing in silver are
very common and often exhibit engine-turned decoration. An
unusual box sought after by collectors of Art Deco is the combined
table box and lighter produced by Tiffany in the 1920s.

*Selection of cigarette boxes from the 1920s: the top one is in gilt-
tooled leather and 6 inches in length; the two centre ones are
cloisonné (left) and in Chinese cinnabar (right), and the bottom one is
black enamel with silver and rhinestone decoration.*

# Cigar boxes

Cigars were introduced into Europe via Spain in the latter half of the 17th century, and the habit of cigar smoking grew popular in Great Britain and western European countries from 1750 onwards.

Most early cigar boxes were in wood, often with japanned or marquetry decoration. They were normally fitted with compartments to prevent the cigars from damage by rubbing together. These were the days before cellophane wrapping! Cigars were among the first items of merchandise to be packaged commercially and many types of container remain today. Others were made of tin with paper transfers or were paper-covered cedar boxes. Cigar cases intended for pocket use came in silver, leather, horn or papier-mâché and were hinged to open in book fashion or had a sliding cover. Papier-mâché examples were common as this was a good material for preserving the cigar and not letting it dry out. Silver cigar cases usually contained single or four cigars and were mostly rectangular with a cigar-shaped outline. In common with snuff boxes and vinaigrettes, some of the best examples were produced by English silversmiths working in the 'toy making' industry of Birmingham.

Cigar dispensers for table use were a Victorian novelty. These are found in many homes today and are mostly made from dark woods, usually rosewood, with a contrasting lighter inlay. They are hexagonal and stand upright, looking somewhat like an old lantern. By turning the knob finial, the six sides open outwards on hinges to reveal the cigars held in brackets on the inside of the doors. Quite an ingenious piece of Victoriana!

There are thousands of general cigar boxes for table use but a very popular American type produced in the decade 1890 to 1900 was in silver plate with a cast finial. It was rectangular in shape, and held 50 cigars and the retail price was 12 dollars and 50 cents!

*Two cigar boxes: in printed tin, 6½ inches long (top) and carved wood (bottom); American, mid-19th century.*

# Tunbridge Ware

Tunbridge Wells in Kent, England, was much favoured in the 18th and 19th centuries as a health resort because of its 'spa' waters. A natural development of this was the growth of a local souvenir trade which, in Kent, centred around the local woodworkers. Visitors would purchase small souvenirs of all kinds, and the boxes in particular retained an enormous popularity owing to their many uses. Card cases, table desks, glove boxes, postcard boxes, money boxes, stamp boxes, were all favourite souvenirs.

Boxes were originally produced in local wood, although later, some more exotic types of imported woods were used for mosaic patterns. Their decoration falls into two categories; early cube and geometric patterns, and later veneered mosaics which became popular from 1845 onwards when this was perfected by a mechanical process. These later productions naturally had more appeal than the cube designs. Cube designs produced in the latter part of the 19th century may include a mosaic border, giving us an idea of the approximate date of the box.

The geometric patterns were produced in multi-colour veneers, often giving a perspective effect, and then glued to a base of rosewood or mahogany. Often the 'ground' would be a veneer on pinewood or other common wood base, and may well have covered the entire surface.

The mosaic designs were produced by a method consisting of cutting thin sticks of various woods and colours according to a pre-set design, clamping them together and then gluing. This produced a wood block, which could be circular or square, or even rectangular, and which, when turned on end, showed the final design or picture to be used to decorate the box or its border. This is known as 'end-grain mosaic', and when cut across a surface to a thickness of about 1/16th of an inch, would enable the manufacturers to repeat the designs on other boxes. The sections were then glued to the surface of the box, sandpapered, and finally varnished. A wide range of mosaic designs were produced, including floral, bird, and butterfly motifs and some landscapes. Few of these boxes are marked by their makers, but occasionally one may have a stamp on the inside of the lid or bear a printed label.

*Selection of Tunbridge Ware boxes with inlaid covers, including a Victorian stamp box 1 inch square (top left); the box shown centre left bears the maker's name of Thomas Barton; all English, mid-19th century.*

# Silver

There are many hundreds of small, useful boxes made not only in silver, but in other metals, such as Sheffield plate, pewter, tin, or brass which are worthy of collection today.

Much thought was given to the production of purses and money cases in the 19th century, and purses in silver, mother-of-pearl, and tortoiseshell glued to a metal base are inexpensive collectors' items today. In the late 19th century, almost all American silver companies made little boxes for various uses, jewellery, powder, soap and so forth. The most popular shapes were simple ovals and hearts, often with an embossed or pierced design in French rococo patterns.

The money case shown is tortoiseshell with piqué decoration in silver, with a central nameplate also in silver, which has been engraved with the owner's initials. The picture also shows a silver coin case in the shape of a heart, made in the second half of the 19th century, and intended to hang from a watch chain. The hinged cover reveals three spring-loaded containers into which the coins slide. Some variations in this type of box allow for compartments for stamps or matches.

The *nécessaire* or *étui* has been used by ladies for centuries. The example shown opposite was made by the London silversmith, Samuel Morden, who specialized in making small boxes, which served as both scent bottle and vinaigrette. This example dates from 1865. The outside of the case is fashioned in the form of a travelling case or portmanteau, and the inside is fitted with small reels for cotton and thread, and a place for needles in the side.

The lancet or scalpel case is in silver with the maker's mark of Taylor and Perry of Birmingham, England. The maker's mark, together with the hallmark, can be seen on the base of the box. The lid is hinged and the interior is fitted with two lancets which have tortoiseshell handles. Such boxes were commonly used until the 1850s.

Matchboxes were mainly produced as novelties and were made in many types of metal, wood, in ivory and porcelain. The silver box shown has two compartments to prevent the accidental firing of the match. After the safety match was developed (from 1830 onwards) boxes were made in a single compartment like the one shown in the shape of a bottle.

Many small boxes for a bewildering variety of uses were made by American companies who specialized in such trinkets, particularly the Sterling Company, Unger Brothers, Gorham Manufacturing Company and Reed and Barton.

*Selection of small silver boxes; the coin case (top right) is 2 inches wide; English, 1800-1900.*

# Decorative enamel

The techniques of enamel decorating have always been highly regarded by collectors of small boxes, *étuis* and ladies' dressing-table boxes.

As early as the 12th century, trinket cases were decorated by one or other of the traditional techniques of enamelling—either cloisonné or champlevé. Cloisonné enamelling involves the technique of laying an intricate groundwork of metal strips (or cloisons) and soldering these on the frame, edgeways up and filling the spaces with enamel. By this method the separate colours are kept apart. This was popular in mid-Europe, Russia and the Orient. The alternative technique, champlevé, involves hollowing small areas in the article and filling these with enamel; this was more popular in western European countries.

Modern enamel boxes are decorated *en plein* mostly with translucent enamel to allow the full effect of the decoration on the individual box to show through. Enamel boxes of the 18th and 19th century have been discussed elsewhere in this book, but enamelling was particularly in vogue during the 1920s and 1930s for both expensive and inexpensive *bijouterie*. Pill-boxes, cigarette cases, *étuis* and powder compacts were all varieties of boxes suitable as gifts for everybody. Expensive enamel boxes made use of gold or silver; they were set with valuable stones, and were made by such famous jewellers as Cartier, Asprey, Van Cleef and Arpels. Arpels produced a particularly useful box which served as an evening-bag called a *minaudière* which had compartments for cigarettes, powder and money. Cheaper kinds were produced in chromium plate. In the 1930s black enamel backgrounds with zigzags and strong geometric designs were favoured and every woman had a powder-box or compact in her handbag enamelled in silver, gold or chrome. Much use was also made of the technique of 'engine turning' which resulted in a repetition of wavy or angular designs and when these were enamelled and polished they produced a ripple-like effect. Inevitable rose-buds and floral bouquets were prevalent and few dressing-tables were without a powder-box in gilded silver or glass with the shining enamel cover so popular in the mid-20th century.

*Enamel 'étui' with plaited strap, 3½ inches long; c. 1920.*

# Dressing-table boxes

Most dressing-table boxes were made in silver, glass or porcelain. The late-19th-century silver box shown is a small replica of a table complete with cabriole legs. The cover is hinged and the centre is plush-lined to contain jewellery or small objects. The decoration is embossed by a die-stamp process with 18th century drawing-room scenes and figures. These are in panels surrounded by heavy scroll work. The process of die-stamping was common on silver dressing-table boxes in the last quarter of the 19th century. Most of these boxes were Dutch but others were made in Birmingham and London. Heart-shaped boxes, ring- boxes, powder boxes etc., were very common and often bore a contemporary Dutch silver assay mark. In addition, those imported into England bear the mark required for all imported silver after 1842. This mark which is a letter 'F' in an oval shield was applied to all silver imported into Great Britain and Ireland until 1904. It is struck alongside the usual hallmark and date letter of the assay office involved. From 1904 the decimal standard of silver was struck and the letter 'F' no longer used. Silver below the ·925 standard could not be marked.

Dressing-table boxes in delicate porcelain have been popular for centuries. Small flower-encrusted boxes from Dresden, the centre of the famous Meissen porcelain works, were highly-prized and copied throughout Europe. Simple porcelain boxes were made in many factories and famous centres were Derby, Coalport and Worcester. The Royal Worcester factory produced miniature boxes decorated with the traditional ivory or apricot glaze, while Royal Crown Derby is renowned for its Japanese patterns painted in deep blue, gilt and iron-red. Coalport is noted for its rose decorations, each picked out in its natural colours. Normally, each of these factories put clear marks on their products but some later 19th-century boxes bore the factory mark of an earlier date. Larger boxes of a finer quality, such as those from the Sèvres factory, were made on the Continent of Europe.

Early American porcelain boxes are very rare, but by the late 19th century, there were a number of factories making decorative ware, including Knowles, Taylor and Knowles, Union Porcelain, and Otto and Brewer. None-the-less, the most popular examples in America were imported from Limoges, Paris, Bohemia and England. On the other hand, silver dressing-table boxes were made by most of the American silver manufacturers, and are sometimes marked accordingly.

*Silver dressing-table box, 4 inches wide; Dutch, 1885 (top) and Sèvres porcelain box; French, 1850 (bottom).*

# Fitted boxes

Among the many kinds of boxes that have virtually outlived their original purpose, the collector can find boxes for razors and straps, brushes, old dressing boxes, lace boxes and general toilet boxes. Nowadays these can be used as good decorative items or can make useful storage containers.

Most early shaving sets were made in silver or wood and were known from the early 17th century onwards. The most fascinating sets were those in silver with fittings that fold away or screw into the top of a small mug to form a shaving set. These were contained in an outer case normally covered in shagreen or leather. They are often called 'campaign' sets; a term which reflects their popular use by military men, and indeed many date from the time of the Napoleonic Wars. Later, travelling razor sets were made in various woods. Ebony cases were common in the mid-19th century.

Another type of fitted box that no longer serves its original use is the apothecary's box, which, from the outside, looks like a decanter box with one or two fitted drawers. Although there are earlier examples, the boxes normally seen date from 1800 to 1850 and were used at home or by doctors when travelling by coach. Mahogany was the most common wood used in their construction and they generally had a rising cover with brass hinges and this enclosed a series of fitted compartments which may number from a dozen to, in the rarer types, over a hundred. Some of these compartments may still house the apothecary's glass bottles with their ground-glass stoppers. If one is really lucky, the bottles may still retain old printed labels indicating the ingredients which today in many cases will seem an unfamiliar medical remedy. The small drawers are also fitted with compartments and often these will still contain the old glass measures, perhaps a small pestle and mortar and a set of old brass scales with their tiny weights to give accurate measurements.

*Wooden inlaid shaving box, 7 inches long (top), maplewood comb and brush box (top centre), and a general-purpose box in pine (bottom); American, 1850-90.*

# Needlework boxes

Every good housekeeper and indeed often the lady of the house in the 18th and 19th centuries possessed a needlework box. These were very personal boxes which might also contain letter-writing accessories since they were very often kept and used in the lady's boudoir.

Most needlework boxes were rectangular in shape and made either of solid or veneered wood. Mother-of-pearl veneer, usually cut in a diamond design, was a popular box covering in the mid-19th century. Small marquetry boxes are quite common but the decoration is usually of poor quality. The cheapest boxes were made of plain wood, usually walnut or rosewood, decorated solely with inlaid strips of box wood.

The most popular boxes were those imported in the late 18th century and throughout much of the 19th century from Japan and China. These were lacquered, wooden boxes, highly polished and usually black, painted in gold with oriental scenes and figures. Such boxes are still quite commonly found and vary in size from 10 inches to 24 inches in width. It is, of course, the interior of these boxes which decides their attractiveness for the collector. Most covers are hinged and the inside fitted either with a sewing pocket, a mirror or a pincushion. The better boxes are silk- or plush-lined and the box is divided into compartments to hold the essential tools of the good needlewoman. A box complete with all its original fittings is quite rare but it can be fun to try and complete the fittings in a sewing box by searching for the missing items. These can often be bought very cheaply. Most needlework accessories are in ivory, bone, or wood although later boxes may include items in papier-mâché and mother-of-pearl. Such accessories would include needlecases for the early steel needles, thread-winders, thread-waxers and holders, thimbles and their cases, shuttles, crochet hooks, reel holders, scissors, and a host of fascinating objects which give insight into the fine handiwork of bygone years.

*Needlework box with compartmentalized interior and original ivory accessories, 14 inches wide; Chinese, made for the European market, late 19th century.*

# Needles and pins

The steel pin as we know it today was an innovation of the middle of the 19th century. Before then, pins were made with a separate top twisting around the pin shaft and many were also covered with black lacquer to prevent rust.

Many ornamental and enamelled pins were produced in the 1880s, and pin cushions made admirable gifts, often sent with a message in embroidery or spelt out in pins on the cushion. Heart-shaped cushions were especially welcomed!

The sentimental Victorian era led to the production of pin cushions and holders with an outer framework of wood, porcelain or silver and a padded centre for the pins. These were often made in the shape of animals, birds, dolls or small figures. The shoe-shaped pin cushion, often elaborately made in silver with red plush lining, was obviously a very popular type judging from the many which remain available for collection. They vary in size from half an inch to 6 inches. If hallmarked, they can be easily dated and many of them were products of the Birmingham 'toy makers'. Pin holders made from old wine coasters are very common.

Needle cases followed similar designs and these were a necessity to protect their contents from rust. Fine needle and bodkin cases in enamels, gold and precious stones have been made for decades as *objets d'art*. Simple needle boxes were also made and there was a profusion of small boxes in ivory, tortoiseshell, Tunbridge Ware and other materials. These date from 1840 through to this century. A particularly charming tortoiseshell variety was made in the shape of miniature knife boxes. Commonly found today are Scottish wooden cases with transfer prints, which were made as souvenirs from a famous resort or spa. Collectors should look out for those needle boxes covered with colour prints made by Thomas Baxter or his licensee, Le Blond. These small boxes with their colourful covers were sold in sets of ten or twelve contained in an outer box. They date from 1850 to 1870. Each set was made up from individual pictures which may still be found on their own and referred to as 'needle box prints'.

'Sewing' châtelaines were made by American silversmiths with hooks for pin cushions, needle boxes, thimble cases etc., all in matching fashionable designs. The little boxes were usually marked only with 'sterling'.

*Horse's hoof mounted as a pin-cushion; American, late 19th century.*

# Japanese lacquer

The lacquer work of Japan is without doubt one of the finest arts in the world. To hold an *inro* which has been decorated painstakingly with suspended gold flecks, to give an aventurine quality, is to admire the patience and skill of a craftsman steeped in the artistic tradition of centuries.

This art was originally Chinese but it spread to Japan well over a thousand years ago and it is Japan that is now considered to be the home of fine lacquer. Most of this work was of fine quality until the end of the 19th century when work of a lesser quality was exported to western countries. Even much of this work is, however, very collectable and provides us with both useful and decorative objects. Particularly attractive are the miniature cabinets containing a series of small drawers which are found in both black and scarlet lacquer.

True lacquer is not just a varnish. It is a material which requires many hours of work to make an object of quality. To give a good, plain, mirror-type black background, an artist would prime the case and apply at least twelve separate coats of lacquer, each of which was polished after drying before a further coat could be added. This was completed before any additional decoration was added which might then require further coats.

The most commonly found Japanese box is the *inro*—a small portable container for seals and medicines, comprising about four or five cases each fitting inside the next. These are drawn tightly together by a silk cord to make them as air-tight as possible. The cords are held together by a bead or *ojime* and the entire object secured to the owner's girdle by the *netsuke*. As there were no pockets in the traditional Japanese dress, such portable *inro* and tobacco boxes were a necessity.

There are many terms used for the various techniques of Japanese lacquer work; for instance *Takamakie* refers to the raised lacquer work found on *inro* and other boxes, giving a dimensional effect and *Togidashi* is the use of gold or silver flecks suspended in many coats of lacquer.

It is important to realize when looking at a lacquer box or *inro* that the decoration reflects the Shinto religion, its folklore and mythology.

*Miniature cabinet decorated in black and gilt lacquer, 12 inches high; Japanese, late 19th century.*

# Snuff boxes

Taking snuff has been fashionable socially since Columbus's day, and some of the finest craftsmanship was devoted to making snuff boxes in gold and enamels set with precious stones. From the 19th century we have been left a legacy of thousands of inexpensive snuff boxes.

They can be found in numerous shapes and sizes and in many different materials. Silver was particularly popular for its property of keeping the snuff fresh and because it made a fine gift. All good snuff boxes have close-fitting lids or covers. Most are pocket-size and, although they may seem clumsy by today's standards, the dress of the period included a waistcoat with pockets large enough to accommodate the snuff box.

The snuff box was very similar in design to the vinaigrette, gilded inside but lacking the inner grilles. Occasionally one finds a double box or one with a dividing section for separating grades of snuff. The 'castle-top' variety of silver snuff box is a very collectable item. These were made by casting from a mould and cover a range of castles including Windsor Castle, Abbotsford House (the home of Sir Walter Scott), Warwick Castle, York Minster, Newstead Abbey, and many others not so easily identifiable. They were popular from 1825 for a period of about thirty years, the best English examples being made by the Birmingham silversmiths such as Nathaniel Mills, Joseph Taylor, Thomas Shaw, Taylor & Perry, Hilliard & Thomason, Edward Smith and other family firms. Each was fully hallmarked with the Birmingham Assay Office mark (an anchor) together with a sterling-silver mark, the date letter, the duty mark of the current sovereign's head and the initial of the original silversmith. The complete silver mark in most boxes is split between the cover and the base of the box, often with the maker's mark appearing on both. Some covers which have been cast exhibit an additional hallmark which is important because it indicates an original separate cast plate inserted into the cover piece. The cheapest type of snuff box is found in black, lacquered papier-mâché often decorated with an ivory or shell inlay.

In America throughout the 19th century snuff continued to be made by tobacco manufacturers, particularly in the Southern States. The boxes for the snuff were usually fairly simple with inscriptions or classic designs in bright-cut silver. Some had sporting prints engraved on the lid, and one type, made especially for boating men, was decorated with beautifully drawn yachts in full sail.

*Snuff boxes in silver and papier-mâché, the centre box 3 inches long, and two silver nutmeg graters (centre right); English, 1800-50.*

# Papier-mâché

Many boxes and caskets in papier-mâché seen today date from the period 1820 to 1860. There was mass production of the material at this time for a variety of products including stationery boxes, compendiums, trays, letter racks, snuff boxes, pen boxes and the like. Indeed, large screens, work tables and chairs were made in papier-mâché which, in its early history, was a true form of 'mashed paper' glued together. In 1772, Henry Clay perfected a paper pulp which used not only paper but wood pulp as well. This improved material was heatproof and could be shaped as required and covered with lacquer varnish which could then be decorated lavishly. Clay's business was established in Birmingham, England, and from this there developed a considerable local industry in lacquer and papier-mâché.

The business was sold in 1816 to the now better-known firm of Jennens and Bettridge, who advanced the techniques of decoration especially using mother-of-pearl as an inlay. For this, the shell was first cut into slivers and glued, as was necessary for the design, onto the body of the article. The lacquer was then built up surrounding the shell and the entire surface was rubbed down with pumice, polished and then baked. These stages were repeated as often as required to perfect the article. On the better articles the shell inlay would be enhanced by hand-painting.

Many, but by no means all, of the pieces from Jennens and Bettridge bear an impressed mark of the firm's name, sometimes coupled with a crown to signify the royal patronage which the company received. Production was continued successfully until the middle of the century when changes in fashion and taste, coupled with a paucity of new designs, caused the firm to close in 1864.

Much papier-mâché was exported to North America and it is surprising that it was not until 1850 that it was made there. A manufactory was established in Litchfield, Connecticut and the work of the skilled European emigrés who made up the labour force of that company is difficult to distinguish from contemporary English products.

*Selection of colourful useful boxes with lacquer decoration, and in papier-mâché; top box 7 inches long; all late 19th century.*

# Painted wood

Early Dutch, Scandinavian, and German settlers in America brought to the country the products of their unique peasant crafts and continued to make the brightly-coloured boxes which they had used in their country of origin for storing utensils, spoons, clothing etc.

Boxes made from ply-wood, varnished and painted with attractive designs, were used for storage and transport of hats, clothing and various personal items. For centuries it was the custom for a prospective bride to receive a bride's box as a gift to store her smaller necessities. Many general-purpose boxes were painted with floral designs; tulips were popular on boxes made in New England and Pennsylvania. Vivid yellows and greens predominate in most cases. Some boxes of better quality have a landscape painting on the cover. I saw an attractive one recently which was rectangular in shape, about 12 inches long, made of ply-wood with a detachable cover which was well painted with an extensive view of the Hudson River. It dates from around 1850. Many of these boxes were used as candle boxes, salt boxes and even playing-card boxes.

Other bright boxes or 'band boxes' were covered in paper and date from about 1830 to 1850; these are usually circular or oval in shape and covered all over with brightly-printed paper showing popular scenes. A good example of this type of box is one dating from this period which records the visit to America of Jenny Lind who was a famous Swedish singer in her day.

*Hat box in plywood with painted decoration, 18 inches high; American, 1830.*

# Pictorial papier-mâché

Most humble papier-mâché boxes were produced for snuff, a habit which became widespread from the middle of the 18th century onwards. This material was ideal; it was cheap and also maintained the snuff at the correct humidity.

Early boxes were rectangular, but the most collectable today are the circular boxes produced from around 1800. Most were British and had pictorial covers. The papier-mâché industry was centred in the Midlands and the best-decorated boxes were those from the workshops of Samuel Raven. He established his business in 1816 after Jennens and Bettridge had taken over the main production of the material. Raven was responsible only for the cover decoration, and he bought blanks from outside for his work. Many of the boxes are painted with portraits in the style of traditional miniatures but somewhat cruder. Like the one illustrated, these are often signed in small red script on the underside of the cover. Other popular boxes were painted with copies of well-known paintings. David Wilkie's 'The Blind Fiddler' was much reproduced. The colours on such copies often make no attempt to match their originals. Some other papier-mâché boxes are decorated in pen and ink or with line-engraved transfer prints. These often take the form of country or inn scenes and the individual processes are difficult to tell apart today owing to the several coats of varnish they received and the wear and tear of years of use. A close examination with a good pocket lens should make the printed covers obvious.

Many similar boxes were made on the Continent of Europe and in Russia, and their decoration—invariably scenes of everyday life—often suggests their source.

Papier-mâché boxes, like enamels, are frequent subjects for erotic art and a cover painted with innocent-looking lovers or religious figures on the outside, may well have more revealing details on the interior!

*Selection of papier-mâché boxes including a circular snuff box, 3 inches in diameter, painted by Samuel Raven (bottom right); English, 1820-50.*

# Jasperware

Jasperware is a highly vitrified stone and was first invented after considerable experiments at Josiah Wedgwood's factory in Etruria, Staffordshire, England. It dates from 1776, and since then a wide range of boxes have been produced, either totally in Jasperware, or incorporating medallions or cameos in Jasperware. Such boxes include patch boxes, *étuis,* snuff boxes, pin boxes, and candy boxes. The body of the material was almost porcelaineous and capable of being coloured right through. This is an indication of true Jasperware. An alternative method was to leave the body white and coat the surface with colour; this method was called 'Jasper dip'.

The early pieces made ideal seals and small portrait medallions. Particularly sought after today are the small cameo plaques and medallions where the decoration is raised in white against a coloured background. They are cut to resemble the classical shell cameo carving and the small plaques were ideal for incorporating into the cover of a small patch box or toothpick case. The first colours were confined to dark blue, light blue, black, green, lilac or yellow. These cameos also decorated such diverse objects as coach-panels, bell-pulls and opera-glasses. Larger pieces of Jasperware were developed in the years after 1785. The product was very successful and was much copied by other Staffordshire makers such as Adams and Turner, and inferior copies emanated from continental sources.

The original Wedgwood, just like today, bore an impressed mark in upper or lower case lettering on the reverse side. If the cameos are mounted on the box cover it may well be impossible to inspect the mark without disturbing the mount and one must judge by the colour of the body and the quality of the cameo cutting. Wedgwood cameos are well-cut with a polished surface.

Wedgwood boxes made entirely from Jasperware and decorated in relief with classical subjects continue to be made in the present day and are a good subject for collecting; most are candy boxes, pin boxes, and small boxes for the dressing-table and are made in a variety of colours in addition to the famous blue-and-white for which Wedgwood is known world-wide today.

*Four 'patch' boxes with covers inset with Wedgwood blue jasper cameos; the centre boxes have gold mounts, and the top and bottom boxes have cut-steel mounts; diameter of circular box 3 inches; English, 18th century.*

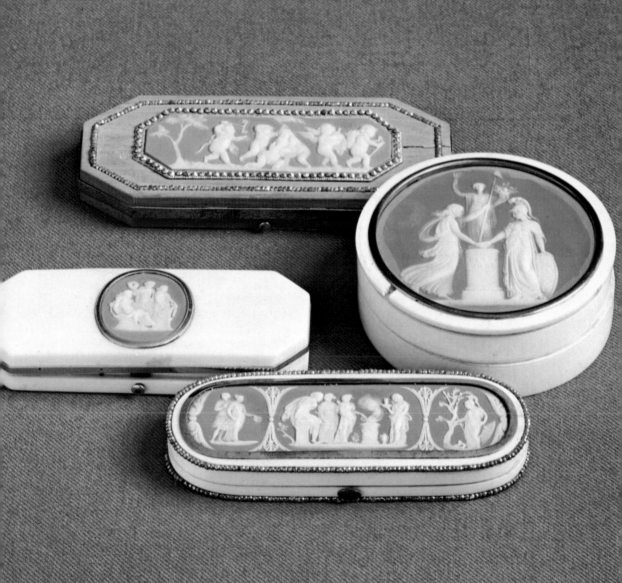

# Utility boxes

Pen boxes, string boxes, tobacco boxes, powder boxes, stamp boxes, glove boxes—these are but a small selection from the myriad of box types which are still available for the collector.

The small box shown (top left) is a general-purpose box with a detachable cover. The carcase is in pinewood, and the whole of the outside and cover is covered in cut porcupine quills. The box dates from about 1825 when quills were still used for writing.

The picture also shows (top centre) a box carved from oak in the shape of a book, and its crude hinges suggest that it was probably made by an amateur.

The octagonal tea caddy (top right) is a souvenir box from the Holy Land. It is made from olivewood, and each panel is carved with a local scene.

The four boxes (centre) are small containers for the dressing-table, suitable for pins, needles, studs and cufflinks. They are all German 'fairings' and were made in cheap hard-paste porcelain, intended to be used as prizes at fairgrounds or to be purchased for a few pennies. They date from the end of the 19th century and were mostly made by the firm Conta and Boehme. They are fairly crude and sparsely decorated with bright enamel colours. Most of them have covers which lift off to reveal a plain interior. They are particularly simple and charming and enhance any collection.

The toilet powder box (bottom left) is a commercial box carrying an advertisement. This is just one of the many types produced in Staffordshire, England, and is decorated by transfer printing and glazing.

Also shown (bottom centre) is an early 20th-century Chinese circular box made in brass with a screw-action cover. It is covered in cloisonné enamels. Many of these were imported from Canton and Shanghai.

The ball-shaped box (bottom right) is a 19th-century string container. String was not sold in balls until about 1820, consequently most boxes must date from the 19th century. Most of them are in turned wood and have a circular aperture, but examples can be found in the shape of barrels, fruit or eggs. Occasionally, the collector may be lucky enough to find one with a cutting blade.

*General-purpose boxes in wood, porcelain and pottery including four 'fairing' boxes, 3 to 4 inches wide; European and Chinese, 1870-1900.*

# Glass

Because of its fragile nature, glass has never been a popular material for boxes, but nevertheless, some decorative boxes have been produced mainly for cosmetic or dressing-table use. The novelty and coloured Art Nouveau glassware of the last quarter of the 19th century is probably the best kind to search out. In England in 1845 a heavy tax on glass was lifted and this encouraged the development of the industry, which mainly centred around Stourbridge. In America, Cranberry glass was developed and produced under licence. The principal centre of American glassware manufacture was the Mount Washington Glass Company whose productions included Satin glass, Burmese glass and Crown Milano.

On the whole, the Art Nouveau glass movement was led by its exponents in France and Austria and today the most sought-after glass is that produced by the designers Emile Gallé, August and Anonim Daum, and the Austrian firm of Loetz. Making boxes was a very small part of their work but the few they did make show the cameo technique which produced decoration in relief. The styles of decoration consist of the typical Art Nouveau swirling plant forms, insects and foliage and most of these products bear a maker's name.

A number of cosmetic accessories were made by Lalique in his easily recognised glass of opalescent blue with moulded decoration. Production of Lalique glass continued after his death and these bear the stamp of the name as opposed to the engraved signature of earlier pieces.

Small boxes were made in the colourful Victorian Cranberry glass, both in America and England. These make good decorative pieces because of their brilliant ruby colouring which can be enhanced by good modern lighting. The original colour was produced by a very small quantity of gold being added to the molten glass.

During this century many cut crystal boxes have been produced for general purposes. Collectors looking for antiques of the future should seek those examples that reflect some decoration or motif relative to their date of production. Crystal cigarette boxes with ashtrays supported by languorous nudes are easily recognised 'bygones' of the 30s.

*Milk glass box with painted decoration and silver mounts. American, early 20th century.*

# Visiting-card cases

In the more leisurely days of the latter half of the 19th century and the beginning of this century, before the wide use of the telephone, etiquette required the presentation of a printed card when calling at a friend's home. Husband and wife would have individual cards which would be left on visits extending welcome to a new neighbour, or on visits expressing thanks for an invitation. Standard etiquette required that such calls should be made between 3 p.m. and 6 p.m. and ought not to last more than a quarter of an hour. Should the lady of the house not be at home, a visiting card was left with the maid. A married lady would not only leave her own card, but her husband's as well.

To carry these cards, some fine cases were made. They were mainly rectangular in shape, about 4 inches in length, and most had hinged covers. They were most commonly made of silver, tortoiseshell, and ivory, but some very expensive ones were made in gold and enamels. Comparatively few were made in wood, although Indian sandalwood, which is a light wood and very suitable for carving, was an exception.

The silver card boxes shown opposite give a brief idea of the many kinds of decoration available to a collector of these cases, ranging from plain bands of engine-turned decoration to finely die-stamped cases in the style of silver snuff box covers. The subjects are often similar to the ones used on snuff boxes; Windsor Castle is a popular one, so is the Crystal Palace, and the Albert Memorial, and several other English scenes which are not so readily identifiable. American designs were more decorative, making use of initials and popular silver patterns, and native flowers and birds. Normally, these were embossed on one side only, but it is possible to find card cases with landscape scenes embossed on both sides. Since card cases did not have the commercial value of snuff boxes, they have in the past been cut up, and the cast or die-stamped ornamentation incorporated in the top of a snuff box instead.

Engraved silver cases vary according to the quality of the engraving. Many popular cases were engraved with a Japanesque design, when the Art Nouveau influence was very strong, and later, silver cases were made which opened in the manner of modern cigarette cases. These often contained more than one division. The cheaper kinds of card case, made from tortoiseshell or ivory, are often decorated with mother-of-pearl.

*Selection of visiting-card cases in silver and tortoiseshell, $2\frac{1}{2}$ inches wide; English, 1880-90.*

# Striking match boxes

In 1826 John Walker of Stockton-on-Tees, England, produced a match which worked by friction. The tip of this match was a composite of potassium chloride and a sulphide antimony which ignited when struck on a roughened surface, such as sandpaper. Walker, however, was not the one to gain any commercial success from his discovery and this came to Samuel Jones who, four years later, marketed the first friction matches in London under the name 'Lucifers'. Early matches were sold in ordinary tins and few of these have survived.

Early boxes originally containing phosphorous matches, however, may still be found and are now collectable items. Phosphorous matches were produced on the continent of Europe in the 1830s and 40s. Although they were easier to ignite than Walker's invention, they had the serious disadvantage of catching light when hot or when placed near heat. Their containers were mostly made in metal but pottery, glass, and wood containers were also produced. Match boxes in the shapes of books, castle turrets, tankards and globes were made.

Friction matches continued to be perfected and were sold in rectangular boxes covered with printed labels, each with a pictorial label or advertisement. Other match containers designed for use on mantelpieces were made in brass, wood or silver-plate in the form of boots or grotesque heads. Match-dispensing boxes with a mechanical action were popular after 1900. They were made of metal, mostly cast iron.

Novelty match-cases or 'vesta cases', as they are also known, were particularly fashionable in the last quarter of the 19th century. Every fashionable Edwardian gentleman wore a heavy pocket-watch across his waistcoat which was not complete without a sovereign case, locket, and fancy vesta case.

In America, match boxes were made mostly between 1890 and 1910, of silver, silver plate, pewter, tin and gutta percha and usually carried the current fashionable design in England and Europe. There were boxes with historical scenes and portraits of American Presidents, there were many with sporting subjects and souvenirs of the world exhibitions of 1876, 1893 and 1904.

*Match boxes: boxes in terra cotta pottery, 4 inches long (top); base-metal box (centre) and lacquer match box, 2 inches long (bottom); American, late 19th century.*

# American trampwork

This strange name, 'trampwork', belongs to a distinctive American folk art involving not only a wide variety of boxes but also such diverse items as mirrors, beds, chests of drawers, plant stands and photograph frames. It is the art of whittling old cigar boxes, vegetable boxes and other softwood boxes with a penknife to make heavily decorated pieces, suitable for home use or ornament.

The classic feature is the angular chip-carving technique employed in conjunction with the layering of the carved wooden sections in diminishing sizes to produce a pyramid effect in high relief. This is shown to good effect opposite.

Chip-carving as a basic form of wood decoration is centuries old and is found in many early European woodwork examples. It was, therefore, a natural choice of decoration for those European immigrants to America in the late 19th century who were unable to find work and eventually became hobos and itinerants. Cigar and fruit boxes were turned into useful articles which could be bartered for food and shelter. Most were small pieces; sewing boxes, jewellery cases were common but larger items may also be found.

There is little documentation of this folk art, but every piece of evidence, such as the dating on newspaper linings and styles of box-lid printing, can be pieced together to form the history of trampwork. Each small box contains its own piece of social history.

*Trampwork box; American, 9 inches high, c. 1850.*

# Tin

Tin boxes suitable for collecting fall into three categories; those which are interesting for their shape or design, those which were produced before advanced printing techniques were developed and those which reflect their social environment. Plain storage tins for commodities such as tea, rice and spices have been in use since the early 19th century. Large-scale packaging of foodstuffs increased in Europe and America from the 1850s onwards. The tin-plate work of South Wales, established in 1801, produced packaging for use in England and abroad. Huntley and Palmer, the biscuit makers of Reading, England, were among the pioneers of tin packaging and it is still possible to come across some of their early tin biscuit-boxes.

The main difficulty with this early tin packaging was suitable decoration on the metal surface. Paper labels were used for early boxes but these were easily torn or affected by damp, and embossing had better effect. They were often stamped with the name of the box makers, or the contents makers, or a royal coat of arms or some similar design.

A marked improvement in box design came with the extension of colour transfer printing onto metal, particularly tin. Many early biscuit boxes, chocolate tins, and cigarette boxes still found in attics and old cupboards today have been decorated by this transfer process. But the process that revolutionized tin-box manufacture was in fact offset printing which was patented in 1875. The basic process is still used today whereby the tin plate to be printed does not directly contact the original lithographic stone; instead an intermediary cylinder is used to 'offset' the design onto the metal.

Some particularly interesting shapes are found in biscuit tins manufactured during the last 75 years. Many show an Art Nouveau influence with curved, tapering bodies and loop handles. The printing of these boxes once again reflects the change in artistic design, but it is dangerous to look for artistic trends in these boxes as their designs did not change so readily as in other applied crafts. Many chocolate boxes and biscuit boxes were produced to commemorate events; coronations and royal weddings are common examples. Still commonly found are the tin chocolate boxes issued to troops serving in the First World War. These are generally gilded bearing embossed lettering.

*Tin boxes for domestic use showing early tin printing; that marked 'snapshots', 10¾ inches high; 1890-1900.*

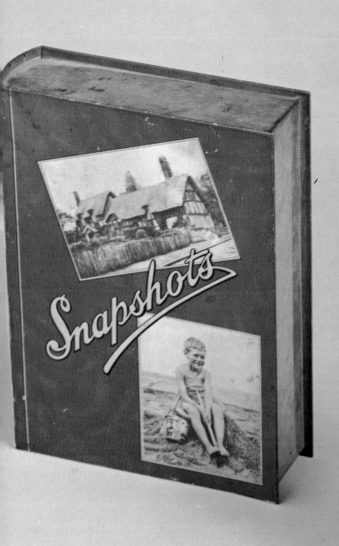

# Enamel

Among the most charming boxes are those produced in 'enamels' —that is, covered by one or more layers of a vitreous substance on a base, usually of copper.

In Europe they were made from the middle of the 18th century. The best known centres of manufacture in England were Battersea; Bilston and Wednesbury in Staffordshire; and, later, Birmingham. The boxes were extremely popular, and exported to countries all over the world, including Colonial America. The Battersea factory existed from 1753 to 1756 and was founded by Stephen Theodore Janssen. The business was not successful and eventually its stock was sold by auction. The enamel industry in the Midlands of England, however, flourished during the last quarter of the century until after the French wars.

The charm of these boxes lies partly in the delicacy and brilliance of the ground colours, which range from a vivid blue to a bright canary yellow, through to the subtle shade of pink known as 'Rose Pompadour'. Boxes may be found in oval, circular, or square forms, or occasionally in the shape of a bird's or animal's head, used for snuff, powder-patch boxes, scent containers or just as souvenirs or gifts. Many have simple quotations engraved on the outside of the cover or, more rarely, on the inside.

The cheaper boxes were not hinged and relied on well-made mounts to form a tight fit. In the cheaper hinged boxes, which were made without mounts, there are normally only three joints in contrast to the five found in more expensive examples.

The invention of a stamping process in 1769 to make the copper bodies did much to cheapen and popularise the enamel box trade. The new method, combined with a dipping process, brought enamel boxes to the general public as souvenirs and gifts from traders. The decoration may range from fine handpainting with expensive gilding to plain transfer printing heightened with some coloured enamel. These cheaper boxes are never signed and one has to rely on colours and shapes for an indication of their origin.

There are some modern firms specializing in copies and 'interpretations' of old enamel boxes, but these are usually clearly marked.

*Group of Bilston enamel 'patch' boxes—note the enamel decoration over the coloured grounds of the two centre boxes, and the transfer printed inscriptions on the plain boxes intended as small gifts; top box $2\frac{1}{2}$ inches long; English, early 19th century.*

Accept
THIS
Present

A Trifle from

LOOE

Take this
for a Kiss

# Wood

The collector can often find useful small containers, in the shape of miniature furniture pieces which can greatly enhance alcoves and dressing-tables. An interesting collection can be made of these miniatures because they imitate the complete range of furniture. Some date from the 18th century but most were made in the last century.

These miniatures are not exactly to scale—the handles are too large for one thing—but they are mainly constructed in the same woods as the 'parent' article. Miniature tables, small lowboys and chests of drawers make acceptable and unusual containers for small jewellery, pins and cuff-links. Many of the pieces were made by apprentices as test-pieces and others were travellers' samples. Often the considerable detail of the original piece is reproduced with inlay, crossbanding or marquetry. It pays to examine the woods carefully; these are often pine or easily-worked fruitwoods which could easily be stained to achieve the colour of a more exotic wood.

Small jewel caskets were often made in rosewood, many with a slightly rounded cover. This strongly figured wood contrasted with the plain ivory bands which were often applied as decoration and, in addition, semi-precious stones such as agate sometimes provided additional 'studded' decoration. Most of these boxes date from 1820 to 1860, are lined with satin, and have a fitted inner tray.

Another storage box which makes an engaging addition to the modern home is the type of dressing box which was exported from China in large quantities in the 19th century. These are often in hardwoods and have little decoration other than applied plain enamel plaques. They fold down to look like plain rectangular boxes, but open up to reveal a fitted mirror or perhaps two fold-away side boxes on swivel pins, above a narrow drawer. They are well made and are still to be bought at reasonable prices.

*Two jewellery caskets, the top one 7½ inches long; American, c. 1900.*

# Scottish boxes

For centuries Scottish craftsmen have made everyday utensils in wood. The Scottish *quaich,* a round drinking vessel, is one of the better-known examples of indigenous craftsmanship.

The Scottish makers of snuff boxes, tea caddies and general-purpose boxes, originally centred at Laurencekirk in Kincardineshire, were well known in the 19th century. The craft later developed in the Ayrshire towns of Mauchline and Cumnock.

Unfortunately, their story is one of development and eventual decline. A handcraft local industry developed at the end of the 18th century producing snuff boxes and small portable boxes. When this trade declined, the craftsmen continued to make souvenir wares decorated by transfer printing.

The principal characteristic of the hand-decorated Scottish snuff box is the hidden hinge, a method of cutting four joints into the base of the box, and three joints in the cover to form a perfectly close fit. The joints were drilled with a hole to enclose a brass hinge-pin which was stopped at each end by a small section of sycamore. The box was then decorated by hand-painting by local artists. The wood commonly used for both the early productions and the latter mass-produced wares was sycamore—much grown in Scotland. The wood, light both in weight and colour, is quite free from knots, which made it ideal for Scottish box-making. It also varnishes easily to a distinctive yellow colour, and has been much used in furniture production as well.

The decline in snuff box manufacture inevitably followed the decline in the social custom of taking snuff. However, the enterprising firm of W. and A. Smith of Mauchline, introduced souvenir boxes from Scotland, which were decorated with Scottish tartans and often identified on the article itself. They were produced from 1820 onwards, and are often found today. The chosen tartan was first painted on paper by a mechanical method and then glued to the sycamore box. Most of these boxes were purchased as souvenirs of visits to leading resorts and the picture subjects later included scenes from all over the British Empire.

*Selection of Scottish wooden boxes, and Tunbridge Ware pictorial box with a view of Eridge Castle, Kent (centre); two snuff boxes, decorated in pen and ink, probably from Cumnock, Scotland (bottom left and right), the smaller one $2\frac{1}{2}$ inches in diameter; all 1820-60.*

# Ivory

Ivory carvings and boxes have been admired products of the Orient for over four centuries. From China came many thousands of ivory objects to please western taste and these ranged from large models of pagodas and pavilions, models of Chinese junks, intricate concentric balls, chess and games pieces, to small counters used for gambling. Many other pieces originally intended purely for Chinese use have been brought back by travellers, including small opium boxes, opium spatulas, snuff bottles and the like. The centre for these export wares was Canton and it was through this port that much of the trading with the West was conducted.

It is not unnatural that the Indian continent, with its native elephant, should produce some fine ivory work. This can be seen in individual carvings and ivory-mounted boxes. In the 19th century much Indian ivory was used for inlay work on general wooden boxes. Travellers to India returned with dressing cases and toilet boxes in addition to the numerous bullock-cart carvings, groups of natives and the famous elephant 'bridges'. General-purpose boxes were often made in sandalwood with detailed inlay consisting of formally-arranged foliage and, in some cases, borders of repeated geometric designs. The boxes vary in size from 6 inches to 2 feet in width. The box illustrated has the pleasing feature of the owner's name inlaid with ivory on the cover.

An important contribution to work in ivory and to folk art has been made by scrimshaw. This is the name given to the carvings produced throughout the last century by lonely sailors and whalemen, both American and British. Most of the work is American, as they had more whalers than the British, but work of British whalers may often be distinguished by the distinctive use of national emblems or flag motifs. Some of this work resulted in useful items, such as small boxes, powder horns, and toys, whilst some was purely decorative. The usual scrimshaw boxes vary in size from 4 to 6 inches and the whalers overcame the problem of jointing by means of overlap straps rather in the manner of Shaker wooden boxes. Several of these small boxes were covered with sealskin and others were made in 'baleen', or whalebone.

*Box inlaid with ivory; Indian, 9 inches long, c. 1875.*

# Early photograph holders

The daguerreotype was the first popular form of portrait photography and soon all fashionable families had their likeness taken. The process is named after Louis Jacques Daguerre (1789-1851) who first presented his technique in 1839. By Daguerre's method each image was produced by the exposure of a silvered copper plate to iodine fumes, developed by mercury vapour and fixed. In early daguer-reotypes, exposure took anything up to 30 minutes but even this hardship did not stop the popularity of the process which by the 1840s had spread throughout Europe and America. To gain the maximum effect, the daguerreotype had to be viewed from an angle. Many were hand-coloured.

These early photographs were treated in much the same way as their predecessors, the painted portrait miniatures, which were kept in hinged frames inside containers made of soft wood, covered with leather and sometimes embellished with a gilt-tooled decoration. The early photograph-holders were enclosed in leather, book-type frames and many are still found with original vulcanite or gutta percha covers or covered with an early plastic material known as *bois durci*. This latter material was a French invention of the mid-19th century and was primarily used for medallions and small snuff boxes. *Bois durci* was used as an alternative to metal, rubber, and wood and was basically a combination of hard wood, sawdust and albumin. After mixing and drying, it was moulded to the necessary shape and placed in a hydraulic press and heated; finally, the substance was immersed in cold water.

The outer surfaces of daguerreotype frames have a variety of mouldings including portrait medallions, floral or musical motifs. Each is invariably contained within a scrolled border. They have a polished finish which looks like polished hardwood. The interiors of daguerreotype boxes are often velvet-lined with a metal frame for the portrait.

Such boxes have remained in circulation mainly to protect an early daguerreotype. However, there will shortly be a time when the cases are collected for their own interest.

*Two daguerreotype boxes in gutta percha and pine, 4 inches long; American, mid-19th century.*

# Writing and stationery boxes

One of the delights of collecting boxes is to be able to use an old box for its original purpose. It is satisfying to use an old wooden writing box to contain correspondence and stamps.

Sloping table desks, either as separate pieces or in one piece of furniture, have been in use for centuries. Portable writing desks or boxes became popular in the latter part of the 18th century and throughout most of the 1800s. The production of suitable glazed writing-paper and the improvement of writing materials, together with the introduction of organized postage, led to the popular demand for a personal writing box.

In general, there are two types; those which look like a rectangular box when closed, and those that form a slope when closed. One of each type is illustrated here.

For the rectangular boxes, exotic coloured woods such as calamander and rosewood were often used, veneered onto a pine base, and brass mounts were added to protect the corners from damage. These consisted either of vertical plates in the more expensive boxes, or of simple screwed-on corner brackets on the cheaper varieties. Most have an interior compartment which is hinged to form a slightly sloping writing surface when opened. Always examine the lock in a writing box, for the quality of the original box is often reflected in the grade or type of lock used. Bramah locks were always used on good quality boxes, and sometimes the name is stamped on the lock.

The interiors of these boxes were fitted with the necessary writer's accessories. Stationery, letters, pen-holders, quills, seals, sealing wax, ink and pounce all had their separate holders or compartments, and many boxes had a secret drawer. Since blotting paper was not commercially produced until 1840, the inclusion of a pounce or sand box in a writing compendium can give an indication of its date.

The type of box which forms a table desk is also illustrated. It has two hinged covers; one opens to reveal the letter rack and inkwell holder, and the other forms the writing surface. This 19th-century box has a veneer in brass and tortoiseshell cut in an intricate scroll design of stylized foliage. This is an example of 'boulle' work, named after André Charles Boulle who was a cabinet-maker in the 17th century, and his technique was much revived in the 19th century.

*Leather portable stationery and writing box, 16 inches wide, and a 'boulle' decorated stationery box; English, c. 1840.*

# Toilet boxes

Fitted travelling toilet boxes and cases are made and purchased today, but some of the finest are those travelling boxes made in the 19th century. From outside they may look like the travelling writing box or work box. The same variety of exotic woods was used, and no doubt they were made by the same manufacturers. Sometimes a writing box was combined with a toilet box, and contained fittings for each use. The difference between the two is obvious when one opens the box; the toilet box invariably has an expensively-fitted interior, often in tiers. The top, removable, tier often contains cut-glass toilet jars and bottles with their engraved silver mounts and covers. These bottles were for cologne, scent and powders, and were usually made in silver; here, for English and American examples, the hallmark or trademark is a useful guide to the approximate date of the box's manufacture. There are also separate holders, and often layers to hold the toilet accessories, such as scissors, steel nail-files, button-hooks and penknives. The inside of the cover may have had a framed mirror, and the base is often fitted with a type of secret drawer released by a spring catch or button on the top of the box inside. Few people could have been deceived by this, however, and it was really intended to prevent the drawer opening whilst the box itself was closed. An alternative to the brass button or catch was the use of a chained brass pin which slid into a retaining hole for the secret drawer.

Wood veneers of strongly-coloured and figured woods such as calamander, rosewood, walnut and mahogany, were used for the outside of the boxes, often combined with brass mounts and trimmings. Brass inlay was used as a decoration rather as it was used in Regency furniture, and indeed many boxes date from this period. The interiors were lined with satin or velvet and the boxes can still serve today as useful, if somewhat bulky, dressing-table boxes. They are often well-made and fitted, and since they are still commonly available, can be recommended as favourable purchases. Their high prices in auction sales and dealers' shops does not really equate with the original maker's price in the 19th century. Yet, this again is a result of the change of social habits. After all, a plastic make-up box is nowadays easier to carry, and much lighter!

*Fitted toilet cases with silver-mounted accessories; English, about 12 inches wide, 1820-80.*

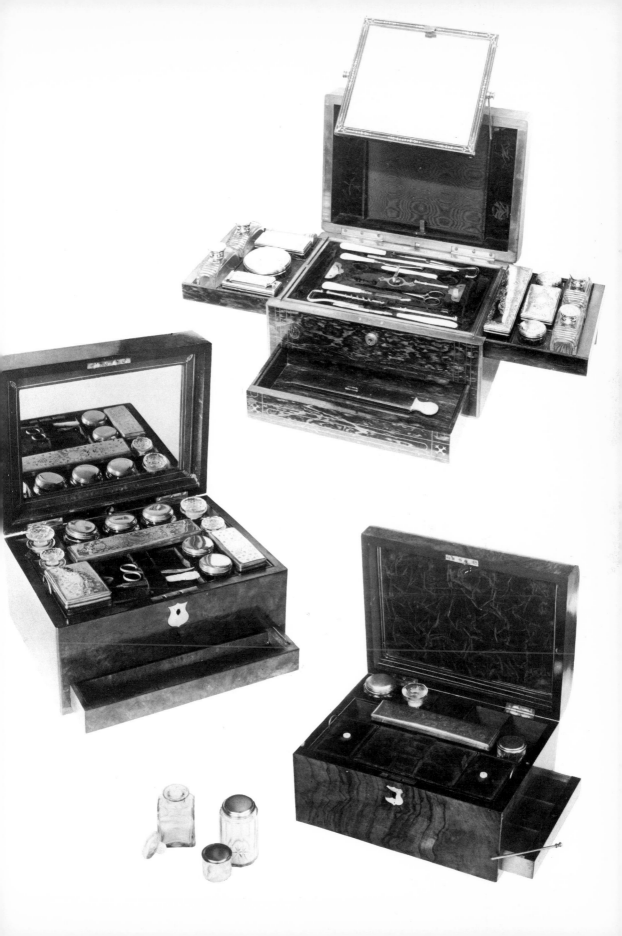

# Vinaigrettes

The purpose of the vinaigrette was to contain a small sponge soaked in an aromatic vinegar which the owner sniffed from time to time in the hope of warding off the evil smells and disease. Even today one can sniff the pungent aroma in the sponge which may still be found in some vinaigrettes.

They were carried on the person either in a pocket or on a chain and for this latter purpose some have small rings. Most are rectangular with a full-length hidden hinge on the back, opening to reveal an interior cover or 'grille' under which the sponge was placed. This grille itself is hinged and in many cases it is pierced in a complex design of arabesques and foliage, but the cheapest examples merely consist of a pattern of pricked holes. To guard against corrosion on the inside it is nearly always gilded.

Most vinaigrettes were made in silver although some rare examples were made in gold. Other materials included hardstones such as agate, which was mounted in gold and silver, and hinged to form a box. The large variety of vinaigrettes can be seen in the wide range of cover decoration and in the shapes and sizes of the boxes. The commonest form of decoration consisted of simple designs of flowers and foliage either hand-engraved or produced by mechanical 'engine-turned' engraving, a process perfected in the first half of the 19th century.

The vinaigrette with the 'castle top' (shown) has a cast cover and is made in silver gilt, the body being of hallmarked silver covered with a thin layer of gold. The decoration is in high relief. It was cast from a mould from which several other covers could then be cast. Similarly, the borders and thumb pieces were cast separately and applied to the finished box.

More unusually, vinaigrettes are found in different shapes such as the simulated book and pocket-watch case shown. Other shapes include acorns, walnuts, telescopes, handbags and cornucopia.

The centre of manufacture in England was Birmingham, although some were made in London and many parts of Europe. Their manufacture was closely allied with the production of silver snuff boxes and makers often specialized in the production of both. American vinaigrettes were most often part of a châtelaine set, and *repoussé* work was particularly popular along with silver-mounted cut glass. They were made well into the 1890s and after.

---

*Open vinaigrette with finely-pierced grille and vinaigrette with pictorial engraving, 2⅞ inches long (top); vinaigrette with cast-cover of 'Abbotsford House', and oval vinaigrette with engine-turned decoration (centre); gold-mounted agate vinaigrette, 'book' vinaigrette, and watch-case vinaigrette (bottom); all English, 1820-50.*

# Art Nouveau

Art Nouveau, the style of the 1880s and 1890s, has a place in box collecting. The artistic influence of such designers as Emil Gallé, René Lalique, Christopher Dresser, Charles Robert Ashbee and Louis Comfort Tiffany can be seen in architecture, furniture-making, ceramics, jewellery, glass and also metal work. As in many inspired movements some of the products became produced on a mass scale leading to debased designs and eventually to the decline of the movement in the early 20th century.

Art Nouveau made free use of plant forms and tendrils, of the graceful flowing curves of the female form and of subtle translucent colours, and concentrated on fine detail. In England many of the designs and products came from the Guild of Handicraft founded in London by Charles Robert Ashbee in 1887. Much patronage was given to it by Liberty and Co. of London. Unfortunately, no designer's marks or signatures were allowed on pieces commissioned by Liberty's and so only attributions can be made. Some of Liberty's silver was inspired by Celtic motifs; this is commonly called 'Cymric Ware' and often bears this stamp. In America, Tiffany led the movement, beginning a little later here, with his renowned glass products. Art Nouveau boxes were mostly made in metal: pewter, copper, brass and silver. These often incorporated semi-precious stones or marble and were decorated by hand.

Much Art Nouveau decoration shows a heavy medieval influence; the brass box shown is an example. The brass is beaten to give a dimpled, hammered surface and hinges and feet are made of separate applied straps. The hinge terminates in two small enamel plaques in the centre of the cover.

Pewter was much used by Liberty's and manufactured under the name 'Tudric Ware' and stamped with this name.

In France, Art Nouveau designers also used pewter to good effect. Much of the cheaper mass produced ware came from Paris and was made in pewter or base metal. These include dressing-table boxes and cigarette boxes of elegant design usually incorporating the female form amidst flower heads and plant scrolls. Often these boxes combine metal work with marble or semi-precious stones as part of the scheme of decoration.

*Art Nouveau boxes: the example top left is 8 inches long; English, late 19th century.*

# 1930s boxes

The Modernist movement in Europe saw the beginnings of artistic design applied to modern industrial production on the scale we know it today.

Modernism in design covered a broad spectrum, from fine art to architecture, furniture, furnishings and all kinds of home decoration. In this manner the late 1920s and 30s gave birth to the new profession of the interior designer and at the same time saw the demise of many individual craftsmen and studio artists who were unable to survive the severe financial depression.

For the immense market of millions of people now available to industrialists, boxes were produced in cheaper materials and were entirely machine-made. Plastics were perfected by leading chemical companies and since the material was non-inflammable and virtually unbreakable it was soon in common use for cigarette boxes, dressing-table boxes etc. Most were made in transparent plastic which could be coloured to choice. The post-Art Deco or Modernist style has a controlled overall geometric design in contrast to the stylised floral designs which typified the preceding decades. Cigarette boxes were one of the most common boxes produced in silver, enamels or ceramics. Wedgwood wares of the era were often matt-glazed in a single colour tone; and many cigarette boxes and ashtrays were made in this material. Glass and mirror-covered boxes were produced in large quantities; a particularly popular powder box which was marketed by Coty was designed by Lalique. This was mass-produced and is easily recognised by the powder puff motif on the cover.

The decline in the employment of household staff, the growth of the cocktail party, the development of the motor car and aeroplane—all these factors changed an age and its social customs and is reflected in the legacy of boxes which remain today.

*Plastic boxes designed for table use, the circular box 4 inches in diameter; English, 1930s.*

# Oriental boxes

Many boxes were imported from the East from the end of the 17th century. These were in porcelain, tortoiseshell, horn, ivory, jade and enamels and most are now collectors' items or museum pieces. By the exacting standard of earlier periods, much of the exported products of Canton and Shanghai were considered too decadent to be worthy of collection and many idealistic collectors retain this view today. By the standards of mass production, however, they were well made and decorated and fortunately many remain for the new collector.

Boxes in Chinese 'export porcelain' were made in very hard paste and were predominantly decorated in *famille rose* enamels. These are the rose pink hues of the figure painting which makes up the panels or 'reserves' and which is surrounded by the border decoration, usually in *verte* or green enamel. The decoration is overglaze and stands slightly raised, in contrast to the blue-and-white pieces where the decoration is underglaze. Emperors, interiors, scenes of tea ceremonies, and figures are frequent subjects.

Canton enamel boxes similarly were debased by export demands of the past century. These, nevertheless, are appealing. They were enamelled on copper, most were circular and had a plain white enamel base allowing further decoration. Again, *verte* and *rose* enamels predominated and the styles of decoration follow traditional lines. On examination, the coloured enamels will be seen to have 'sunk' into the body enamel during the later firings and do not appear in relief as in the case of porcelain enamels.

Until the early 20th century, Japan also exported boxes which were made of a 'debased' type of lacquer work, merely a heavy varnish or painted lacquer. Nevertheless, many delightful boxes were made and exported. Two examples are the *suzuri-bako,* used for calligraphy, and the *ko-ju-bako,* a box containing a nest of smaller boxes.

*Selection of Oriental boxes: a lacquered horn cigar case, about 6 inches long, four silver opium boxes and an enamel cylindrical box; Chinese, 1850-80.*

# Tea caddies and chests

The term 'caddy' is derived from the old Malayan word '*Kati*', denoting a specified weight, equivalent to about $1\frac{1}{4}$ lb. Originally, boxes were made to contain that amount of tea. These were placed in outer containers of wood which were sometimes covered with leather shagreen, a popular material of the mid-18th century. Eventually, the need for outer containers diminished and the interior box became the individual caddy.

Since taking tea was an important custom, to have the correct caddies and equipage was a social necessity. The great names of English cabinet-making such as Thomas Chippendale, George Hepplewhite, Robert Adam and Thomas Sheraton all designed tea caddies. Tea caddies of the mid-18th century are found in solid mahogany with carved decoration. Wooden caddies from the latter part of the century may have two divisions or just a single compartment, and are customarily made in the lighter woods favoured at the time, e.g. satinwood and stained sycamore. These were decorated with a marquetry inlay sometimes in a classical design, or with shells, husks or painted panels. Nearly all caddy covers were hinged and fitted with locks. The inner compartment was sometimes divided into two with a glass bowl dividing the two containers, to be used either for mixing the grades or types of tea, or to contain sugar.

Another popular variety was the turned-wood caddy in the shape of fruit. These were often made in the wood of the simulated fruit, were hinged at about three-quarters of their height, and the interior was foil-lined. Caddies of the 19th century were often of a classical rectangular form or 'sarcophagus' shape. They may be veneered wood or have veneers of tortoiseshell or ivory, and be either plain or inlaid with silver, pewter or mother-of-pearl. At the turn of the 19th century, caddies were also made in curled paper or quillwork. These were basically made of deal with recessed panels which surrounded a painted or inlaid central motif, and the panels were filled with tiny rolls of coloured paper to form a design around the motif.

There were comparatively few tea caddies made in America although Paul Revere made at least one to match a tea service. There are a few other examples up to about the turn of the century, but these are fairly rare and were probably only made to match tea sets.

*Tea caddies in tortoiseshell, fruitwood and ivory inlaid with silver: the fruitwood example is the size of an apple; English, 1800-50.*

# Decanter boxes

It was the Roman glassblowers who discovered that square bottles were easier to pack, and safer in transit than round shapes. Early cases for bottles were made of leather thongs, or straw and rope, much as Chianti wine is still carried today. As travelling became more comfortable and convenient, it became necessary to find a more attractive way of transporting the wines, liquors, spirits and other necessities of 'civilized' life.

In the days of coaches, the traveller often needed to fortify himself for the long journey ahead, or, during the journey, to 'lay the dust' by means of a tot of spirits. The spirits were contained in cut-glass decanters which were usually square in shape and thus fitted easily into a container or decanter box. These boxes are mostly quite unpretentious from the outside, but show good joinery work inside. The box shown opposite consists of a pine base with a mahogany veneer, and the dome lid has room to accommodate the original drinking glasses. Larger boxes are still sometimes found fitted not only for decanters and glasses, but for wine and spirit bottles as well. These fell out of favour when the 'tantalus' with its locking frame was introduced in the mid-19th century.

None-the-less, there are still Victorian versions of a drinking man's picnic basket, with fittings for every possible addition to liquid refreshment—corkscrew, mixer, small bottles for spices, lemon peeler, different sorts of glasses, etc. The interiors were often covered in velvet or fine leather, with little straps and loops to hold everything in place. Sometimes the box itself would be quite elaborate, with inlay and brass handles, and initials in brass or silver. Others were more practical and often suffered damage on the corners, if the owner was a popular guest.

Although many decanter boxes are now found without the interior fittings, it is an interesting pastime to try and purchase old spirit decanters which would fit these boxes and they certainly look attractive on the modern sideboard.

*Georgian mahogany liqueur decanter box; English, 10 inches wide, c. 1820.*

# Mother-of-pearl

All collectors of boxes should endeavour to include at least one example of mother-of-pearl in their collections. In the hands of a good craftsman it can be shown to superb effect, displaying a radiant iridescence.

The best material comes from the lining of the oyster pearl. It was mainly used as a veneer on jewellery boxes, visiting-card cases, match boxes, tea caddies and snuff boxes etc. Occasionally, it is to be found in larger single pieces forming the top and base of the box, such as a cachou, bonbon, or patch box. In this form the mother-of-pearl may often be carved with figures or landscapes. Here, the framework of the box may be in silver or Sheffield plate, and is usually devoid of the customary collection of hallmarks to be found on silver, which presents some difficulty in dating.

Mother-of-pearl was not the only type of shell to be used in snuff boxes, and boxes made from the whole conch shell measuring some $2\frac{1}{2}$ to 4 inches are quite common. They have a metal mount which serves as a hinged cover made from a non-precious metal.

When used as a veneer, the mother-of-pearl can be sawn, filed or carved to the craftsman's choice. When a whole surface was to be covered the mother-of-pearl was usually cut in diamond or square patterns and firmly glued to the whitewood base. The material was often used on its own, as in the fine jewel casket shown opposite, or in conjunction with the somewhat similar materials, tortoiseshell and ivory. The final surface was then highly polished to emphasize the rare and radiant natural effects of the material.

*Jewel casket veneered in mother-of-pearl (top); tortoiseshell scent bottle case, $7\frac{3}{8}$ inches long, tea caddy veneered with mother-of-pearl, and small shagreen and silver mounted box (right); four match cases with varying mother-of-pearl and tortoiseshell decoration (bottom); all English, late 19th century.*

# Bibliography

BEDFORD, J. *All Kinds of Small Boxes.* New York, 1964.

BERRY-HILL, H. and S. *Antique Gold Boxes.* London, New York and Toronto, 1960.

BRAMSEN, B. *Nordiske Snusdaser.* Copenhagen, 1965.

DELIEB, E. *Silver Boxes.* New York, 1968.

FREDERIKS, J. W. *Dutch Silver,* vols II and III. The Hague, 1958, 1960.

HONEY, W. B. *Dresden China.* London, 1934.

HUGHES, G. B. *English Snuff-boxes.* London, 1971.

HUGHES, T and B. *English Painted Enamels.* London and New York, 1951.

KLAMKIN, M. *The Collector's Book of Boxes.* Newton Abbot and New York, 1970.

LE CORBEILLER, C. *European and American Snuff-boxes 1730-1830.* London, 1966.

NOCQ, H. and C. D. *Tabatières, boîtes et étuis . . . du Musée du Louvre.* Paris, 1930.

PINTO, E. H. *Wooden Bygones of Smoking and Snuff-taking.* London, 1961.

PINTO, E. H. *Treen and Other Wooden Bygones.* London, 1969.

RACKHAM, B. *Catalogue of the Schreiber Collection,* vol III. London, 1924.

SNOWMAN, A. K. *Eighteenth Century Gold Boxes of Europe.* London, 1966.

SNOWMAN, A. K. *The Art of Carl Fabergé.* London, 1953.

UKHANOVA, I. N. *Russkie laki v sobranii Ermitazha.* Leningrad, 1964.

WATSON, F. J. B., and DAUTERMAN, C. C. *The Wrightsman Collection,* vol III. New York, 1970.

# Picture acknowledgements

Page numbers given, those in italics refer to colour.

Christopher Sykes Antiques, Woburn: 13, *15*. Lee Berman, Little Neck, New York: 17, *31, 75,* 77. Sheila and Daniel Nilva, New York: *19,* 25, 51, *89.* Phillips the Auctioneers, London: 21, *81,* 97, 103. Collection of Mr A. Ball: *23,* 69. The Place off Second Avenue for Antiques, New York; Lee Berman, Little Neck, New York: 27. Lee Berman, Little Neck, New York; Sheila and Daniel Nilva, New York: *29,* 83. Collection of Mr A. Ball; Edwin Smith: 33. Privately owned: *35, 53.* The Place off Second Avenue for Antiques, New York: 37, 55. The Meating Place, Port Washington, New York; The Showcase Antiques, Great Neck, New York: *39.* Tiger Trading, New York; Then Antiques, Great Neck, New York: 41. Penny Waterhouse, Antiquarius, London: *43.* Collection of Mr and Mrs P. Wyer: 45, 59, *95.* The Meating Place, Port Washington, New York: *47.* Collection of Mrs M. Cole; Baroness Barth von Wehrenalp: 49. Lelac Antiques, London: *57.* The Meating Place, Port Washington, New York; The Showcase Antiques, Great Neck, New York; Lee Berman, Little Neck, New York: *61.* Then Antiques, Great Neck, New York: *63.* City Museum and Art Gallery, Birmingham: 65, *85,* 101, *107.* Josiah Wedgwood and Sons Limited, Stoke-on-Trent (Wedgwood Museum, Barlaston Collection): *67.* Gloria B. Silver, New York: *71.* Mrs M. Cole: 73. The Place off Second Avenue for Antiques, New York; Sheila and Daniel Nilva, New York: *79.* Privately owned; Phillips the Auctioneers, London: 91. Mrs J. Worthington: 87. Mrs J. Worthington; Gavina Ewart Antiques, Stratford-on-Avon; privately owned: 93. Dan Klein Antiques, Islington: *99.* Mr and Mrs J.R. Williams: 105.

The following photographers were commissioned to take photographs for this book:
A.R. Teugels, Art Camera, Kingston-upon-Thames: 13, *15, 53,* 91 (top).
Bob Shewchuk Productions, New York: 17, *19,* 25, *27, 29, 31,* 37, *39,* 41, *47,* 51, 55, *61, 63, 71, 75,* 77, *79,* 83, *89.*
Neville W. Smith, Stratford-upon-Avon: *23,* 33, 45, 49, 59, 65, 69, 73, *85,* 93, *95,* 101, *107.*
A.E. Coe, Norwich: *35.*
A.C. Cooper Limited, London: *43, 57, 81, 99,* 105.

# Index